THE NAPOLEONIC EMPIRE

GEOFFREY ELLIS

MACMILLAN

First published 1991

Published by
MACMILLAN EDUCATION LTD
Houndmills, Basingstoke, Hampshire RG21 2XS
and London
Companies and representatives
throughout the world

Printed in Hong Kong

British Library Cataloguing in Publication Data
Ellis, Geoffrey
The Napoleonic empire. – (Studies in European history).
1. France. Napoleon I, Emperor of the French, 1769–1821
I. Title   II. Series
944.05092
ISBN 0–333–42047–0

Series Standing Order

If you would like to receive future titles in this series as they are
published, you can make use of our standing order facility. To place a
standing order please contact your bookseller or, in case of difficulty,
write to us at the address below with your name and address and the
name of the series. Please state with which title you wish to begin your
standing order. (If you live outside the United Kingdom we may not
have the rights for your area, in which case we will forward your order
to the publisher concerned.)

Customer Services Department, Macmillan Distribution Ltd
Houndmills, Basingstoke, Hampshire, RG21 2XS, England.

Contents

Editor's Preface   vii
A Note on References   viii
Preface   ix
1 Introduction: Napoleon in Historiography   1
2 The Inheritance   8
   (i)   The evolution of a military career   8
   (ii) The evolution of a revolutionary state   12
3 The Civil Foundations of the Napoleonic State   18
   (i)   Central, departmental and local government   19
   (ii) The '*ralliés*' and the opposition   28
   (iii) The financial reforms   33
   (iv) The Concordat and Church–State relations   39
   (v) Justice, the Napoleonic codes, and education   44
   (vi) Summary   48
4 The 'Grand Empire' and the 'Grand Army'   50
   (i)   Territorial and dynastic aggrandisement   50
   (ii) The military establishment   54
   (iii) Napoleonic warfare   64
5 The Formation and Endowment of an Imperial Élite   73
   (i)   Nobles and *notables*   73
   (ii) The treatment of the annexed lands and
       subject states   82
6 The Imperial Economy   94
   (i)   Agriculture   94
   (ii) Aims of the Continental Blockade   95
   (iii) Effects of Napoleon's economic policies   99
7 The Legacy   107
Appendices   114
Maps   119
Glossary   121
Select Bibliography   124
Index   137

For Patricia, substantially

Editor's Preface

The main purpose of this new series of studies is to make available to teacher and student alike developments in a field of history that has become increasingly specialised with the sheer volume of new research and literature now produced. These studies are designed to present the 'state of the debate' on important themes and episodes in European history since the sixteenth century, presented in a clear and critical way by someone who is closely concerned himself with the debate in question.

The studies are not intended to be read as extended bibliographical essays, though each will contain a detailed guide to further reading which will lead students and the general reader quickly to key publications. Each book carries its own interpretation and conclusions, while locating the discussion firmly in the centre of the current issues as historians see them. It is intended that the series will introduce students to historical approaches which are in some cases very new and which, in the normal course of things, would take many years to filter down into the textbooks and school histories. I hope it will demonstrate some of the excitement historians, like scientists, feel as they work away in the vanguard of their subject.

The format of the series conforms closely with that of the companion volumes of studies in economic and social history which has already established a major reputation since its inception in 1968. Both series have an important contribution to make in publicising what it is that historians are doing and in making history more open and accessible. It is vital for history to communicate if it is to survive.

R.J. OVERY

Note on References

References are cited throughout in square brackets according to the numbering in the general bibliography, with page references where necessary indicated by a colon after the bibliography number. Where the same reference gives more than one bibliography number, the latter are distinguished by commas.

Preface

This booklet was commissioned and outlined in rough draft while I was the Oxford Visiting Professor at the University of South Carolina, Columbia, during the spring semester of 1984. During that time I had the privilege of working closely with Professor Owen Connelly, America's foremost Napoleonic scholar, and of chairing his excellent graduate seminar on the French Revolution and Napoleonic Era. The Program Committee over which he presided shortly afterwards invited me to chair a plenary session at the annual conference of the Society for French Historical Studies which met at the same university in March 1988. On that occasion I also had the pleasure of introducing Professor Louis Bergeron as one of the guest speakers.

My readers will soon recognise the debt I owe to the published works of both these scholars, although the bibliographical requirements of the present series allow me to note them in only a very general way. Professor Bergeron's doctoral thesis, articles and textbook (*France under Napoleon*) have greatly influenced my own approach to Napoleonic history. A similar debt to Professor Connelly's earlier works was reinforced when his *Historical Dictionary of Napoleonic France* appeared just as I was preparing my final drafts. This enabled me to check a good many facts and bibliographical references before going to print. I should like to acknowledge in full measure all I owe to the scholarship of both professors and to thank them for their generous help and encouragement. I also hasten to dissociate them from any shortcomings of this work.

G.J.E.

1 Introduction: Napoleon in Historiography

The best introduction to the changing images of Napoleon in historiography since 1815 remains Pieter Geyl's classic, *Napoleon: For and Against*, first published in 1949 [22]. Ranging from the earliest apologists and critics of the emperor to the interwar writers of this century, it offered much the finest synthesis of earlier interpretations of Napoleon's achievement. The author's very personal experience of the Second World War and analogies with another conquest of western Europe and failed invasion of Russia gave his account a tendentious quality of unusual interest. If its comparison with Hitler's *Reich* made Napoleon's impact on Europe appear altogether less vile and destructive for the subjugated peoples, Geyl nevertheless admitted that his sympathies lay 'with the *against* rather than with the *for* category'. All the major themes of Napoleonic historiography, of both the real and the legendary emperor, came into his focus. He set out skilfully whatever good or bad Napoleon had done, or had been thought to have done. He was thoroughly at home with the polemical as well as the scholarly literature on the subject, and his book not surprisingly found its way into subsequent paperback editions.

Yet Geyl had intended to write, as he put it, 'a book on Napoleon as seen by French historians'. Since he did so before the new critique of Napoleonic social and economic history came into its own, his views were not influenced by the ways of the modern computer and its burgeoning '*équipes*'. In that sense at least his account is rather 'dated' now. In the past thirty years or so the subject has moved from studies in the cult of personality, or from the deeds

1

of war and conquest, to the longer-term underlying structures and mentalities of the Napoleonic Empire. The most important recent research in this field has concentrated on its institutional and more particularly its social and economic history. The effect has been to stress the continuities quite as much as the changes in French society from the Revolution to the First Empire, and indeed beyond it. This new genre of Napoleonic studies, already evident during the preceding decade, had its first collective airing at the Sorbonne conference of October 1969 which marked the bicentenary of Napoleon's birth [14]. Its leading themes have since been widely developed by scholars in France and in other countries, notably West Germany and Italy, and are discussed more substantially in later chapters of this booklet.

Such research into the social and economic structures of the Empire has led, in turn, to important reappraisals of Napoleon's aims and ambition as well as of the long-term effects of his rule. So far, however, its major currents have not been channelled into English textbooks, which still deal largely with the more familiar military and political aspects of the subject, or else perpetuate our old infatuation with the private lives of the Bonapartes. For English readers, the translation of Georges Lefebvre's old masterpiece in the 'Peuples et Civilisations' series remains a basic source [24]. The most accessible introduction to the present state of Napoleonic studies is also through translated works. One of these is Louis Bergeron's *France under Napoleon*, an excellent digest of his major research into the economic, social and cultural history of the period [16]. It covers at least some of the ground of his important doctoral thesis on bankers, merchants and manufacturers in Paris from the Directory to the Empire [144], of his articles on the same broad topic, and of his works (some in collaboration with other authors) on the Napoleonic *notables*. Another useful source is Jean Tulard's *Napoleon: The Myth of the Saviour*, whose wide range includes a good synthesis of his other major contributions to the social history of the period [32].

The last two cited works are valuable additions to

2

school and university libraries, offering as they do interesting and up-to-date reinterpretations of the matter in older writings, along with the communication of new research. The approach of both authors might also be called 'revisionist' in the sense that they apply empirical methods to old polemical shibboleths in reappraising the familiar image of Napoleon as a radical reformer. One of the merits of Tulard's book indeed is that it distinguishes the 'myth' from the 'reality' in earlier accounts. Reviewed in this light, the social effects of Napoleonic rule now seem more conservative than was once thought. Bergeron's account deals mainly with institutional and socio-economic structures, including what it is now fashionable to call the 'mentalities' (*mentalités*) of the period. Following the requirements of the series in which it appears, it is not much concerned with the wars of conquest or the treatment of the subject states. These are partly covered in a companion volume on the foreign aspects of Napoleonic rule, as yet untranslated and certainly much less original [25]. Tulard's text has more to offer in linking narrative with commentary, but with its notes is over 400 pages long, and unfortunately the English translation is riddled with howlers.

Among other works available in English, two in particular offer the general reader a representative sample of the mass of original documentary sources. The old edition of Napoleon's letters by J.M. Thompson [6] is probably still the most accessible short cut to the marathon series published during the Second Empire by Napoleon III [5]. It might be read in conjunction with J. Christopher Herold's fascinating selection from the written and spoken words – the 'mind' – of Napoleon [2]. Of the general textbooks published in Britain or the United States, the most useful remain the clear and well-informed accounts of Felix Markham [27] and Owen Connelly [19, 20]. The last named had already given us an important introduction to Napoleon's satellite kingdoms [120], and has also published an excellent reassessment of the military campaigns [96]. His recent dictionary of Napoleonic France, which assembles the expertise of scholars from several countries, is certainly the most authoritative available in English [10]. Irene Collins has followed up her very readable study of the Napoleonic 'parliaments' and their personnel [38] with a pamphlet of more general range in which the main issues of current research are briefly discussed [18]. A few years ago, in an essay on the Napoleonic élites, I gave my own introductory statement on the social question [108], having already dealt with the economic aspects in a monograph on the Continental Blockade [154].

Otherwise, the absence of a general synthesis in English has isolated our students from the mainstream of current Napoleonic research abroad. Our knowledge and understanding of Napoleon's impact on France and on Europe remains old-fashioned, lop-sided, and is now increasingly mistaken. So far from coming up with fresh answers, we appear not even to be asking the sort of questions which historians across the Channel have been doing for some thirty years. The major contribution of English-speaking historians to research on the old regime and the French Revolution, at once apparent in the bibliographies of the earlier volumes by William Doyle and T.C.W. Blanning in the present series, has not yet extended to the Napoleonic period. And so, if much of what follows in this booklet may seem unfamiliar, or perhaps even perverse, readers should note that it has already been widely argued in France and in other continental countries.

The emphasis here is therefore on more recent research otherwise unfamiliar or inaccessible to the English general reader. A volume of the present size and format on the whole of Napoleonic Europe, covering all the annexed territories, the subject and allied states, as well as France, would have been over-ambitious. I have preferred a view of the broader picture *from* France, as it were looking outwards to conquered Europe. It seemed appropriate, first, to concentrate on France and the lands directly annexed to it, which from May 1804 formed the official area of the Empire, and which at its height in 1811 had 130 departments and over 40 million subjects. The perspective then widens to include the satellite states beyond the Imperial frontiers which from 1806, at least,

4

became integral functions of Napoleon's policies. At issue here are his dynastic designs, the link between his social promotions in France and his land-gifts in Italy, Germany and Poland, and the extension of his Continental Blockade or 'System' to that wider imperium. In this way his achievements and failures in the so-called 'Grand Empire' can be related more closely to those in France itself.

Such an approach raises three central questions: the nature of Napoleon's aims and ambition, the 'mechanics' of his policies as actually applied, and lastly their effects in both the short and long term. In the light of recent research into all these questions, a new picture of the emperor and of his work is forming. For a long time it was traditional to ask the old chestnut of a question: was Napoleon the heir of the Revolution? The older textbooks have had their say on the matter; yet, interestingly, the question *can* now be asked and answered afresh. We have, for instance, much more information on the military theme, on Napoleon and his closest associates as career-soldiers; on the continuous adaptations of social and professional élites within the legal framework of the Revolutionary land settlement and the institutions of the Napoleonic state; and on the economic fluctuations over nearly a quarter of a century, in which France indeed conquered the land but practically lost all command of the sea.

In a memorable phrase Bertrand de Jouvenel once remarked that 'Napoleon was master in Europe, but he was also a prisoner there' [159: *191*]. His priorities were essentially Europocentric, for if his power was land-based, it was also land-locked. It is within the *continental* dimension of his rule, not in the dreams of maritime and global empire, that we shall find the essential Napoleon, the emperor of deeds. That is where his impact was most immediately felt and where it lasted longest. But even within this continental sphere, the hard base of his military domain, the civil effects of his rule were not always as radical and innovatory as has often been supposed. The letter of the Imperial law, the terms of the Napoleonic codes, and the constitutions formally proclaimed in the subject states all

5

suggest a reforming zeal of colossal scale. In practice, however, not all of that reforming vision was systematically carried through to its official conclusion. The explanation lies partly in Napoleon's constant military needs, notably for cash, and partly also in the varying time-lags through which the several conquered lands were exposed to French rule. If his great codes and other civil reforms anticipated the professionalisation of later political systems, his military, dynastic and social designs had more in common with the mentality of earlier warrior-kings. Bergeron states the paradox nicely: 'Napoleon was both behind and ahead of his time, the last of the enlightened despots, and a prophet of the modern State' [16: *xiv*].

Granted this, celebrated motifs which once subsumed the nature of Napoleon's ambition – Émile Bourgeois' 'oriental mirage' [17], Édouard Driault's 'Roman ideal' [21], or more grandiloquently still the 'universal empire' which some, like Thiers [31], have seen as his ultimate aim – now seem unreal. They are part of the 'myth', of the legend so colourfully cultivated on St Helena by Las Cases [3] and by later Napoleonists, but they have little basis in fact. Of all the symbolical images of Napoleon's true ambition, as recounted in the long historiography on the subject, the 'Carolingian' analogy remains the most plausible. Indeed, Napoleon self-consciously encouraged this vision of himself as a 'new Charlemagne' and of his realm as the historic heir of the old Frankish Empire, extending naturally from France into Germany and Italy. It is not only the ceremony of his Imperial coronation, when he flaunted the sword and crown of Charlemagne as symbols of his inheritance, that recalls this analogy. Of greater significance was his more practical, indeed more practicable, interest in a 'German' and an 'Italian policy'.

Some notable historians like Charles Schmidt and Marcel Dunan were among the first to argue the Carolingian analogy in their detailed accounts of Napoleon's work in Germany [134, 125]. They saw the old Lotharingian ideal, the 'middle kingdom' or 'third Germany' which would hold the balance between Habsburgs and Hohenzollerns, fading before an ominous new vision of German confederation under Napoleon's domination. Cast in this light, the vitality of the German peoples would serve the Imperial might and grandeur of France in the form of military auxiliaries and economic vassals. Dunan even argued that, outside France, Napoleon's 'grand idea' was the reorganisation of Germany, and that this was the main function of his wider preoccupation with 'the English question' after 1806. German historians were quick to pick up the analogy, too, and the fullest statement of the argument in that language is still to be found in the work of Hellmuth Rössler [29].

The Carolingian motif appropriately stresses the essentially Latin and Teutonic bases of the 'Grand Empire'. To it we should add another, emerging picture of Napoleon as the last of the old war-lords of Europe, who for military, fiscal and social reasons, rather like the enlightened despots before him, made his practical compromise with feudal structures in the conquered lands. Part of my purpose here is to explain the aims of that policy and to assess its impact on France and her satellites. In particular, I hope to establish a close organic link between Napoleon's system of social honours in France itself and his treatment of the subject states in Italy, Germany and elsewhere, from which so much of the wherewithal was derived.

2 The Inheritance

(i) The evolution of a military career

There is still one country in Europe which is fit to receive laws, and that is the island of Corsica. The valour and fidelity with which this brave people has recovered and defended its freedom entitle it to be taught by some wise man how to preserve that freedom. I have a presentiment that this little island will one day astonish Europe.

So wrote Jean-Jacques Rousseau in his famous tract, *The Social Contract*, of 1762 [8]. His 'presentiment' could hardly have been fulfilled with greater irony. From Corsica during the next few decades there was indeed to come a law-maker, a man of valour, and in his own way a man of fidelity too. But whether he was destined to recover freedom for his native shore, or to bring it to the mainland of Europe, raises a question of definition on which Rousseau, who died in 1778, would surely have had a lot more to say.

The territory of France had increased in the course of the seventeenth and eighteenth centuries, and among her acquisitions had been the island of Corsica, annexed in 1768 by Louis XV after a commercial deal with its former rulers, the Republic of Genoa. Napoleone Buonaparte was born there in the capital, Ajaccio, on 15 August 1769. As a youth he was a beneficiary of the king's amnesty to former Corsican rebels against Genoese rule. His father accepted the amnesty, and in 1770 his status as a petty noble was recognised under French law. This made it possible for Napoleon, the second of eight children of Carlo Buonaparte and his wife, born Letizia Ramolino, to be educated on the

French mainland at royal expense. The 'family' aspect of Napoleon's career intrudes even at this early stage. If blood is thicker than water, then the Bonapartes are a striking example of the phenomenon. In the most serious study of Napoleon's relations with his family ever attempted, Frédéric Masson argued that the emperor was moved by a 'clan spirit', itself typical of Corsican custom, which he later turned into a grandiose policy of 'housing the family' (*caser 'la famiglia'*) on the satellite thrones of Europe [28]. The insecurity of it all was to be captured by Letizia, the future 'Madame Mère', in her instinctive remark: 'if it only lasts' (*et si ça dure*).

Napoleon entered the military school in Brienne at the age of nine, then transferred to the École Militaire in Paris, where he passed in 1785 as a sub-lieutenant of artillery at the age of sixteen. During the three or four years preceding the Revolution his artillery training was extended first in the Régiment de la Fère at Valence, where he was commissioned as a lieutenant, then at the military school of Auxonne (1788–9). The emigration of many noble commissioned officers during the first two or three years of the French Revolution – as many as 60 per cent (some 6000) by August 1792 – opened up careers for a new generation of talented junior commissioned officers and NCOs, as France went to war with Austria and Prussia (from April 1792), then with Britain, Holland and Spain (February–March 1793) [90, 102]. Napoleon was one of this new breed of risen career-soldiers, who had had their early training in the military academies of the old regime, and who were to be projected into spectacular success and professional advancement during the wars of the Revolution. Such astonishing careers would no doubt have been unlikely and perhaps even unthinkable for petty nobles and commoners in the venal system of military promotions current under the old regime.

After serving briefly as a first lieutenant with the Régiment de Grenoble at Valence in 1791, Napoleon was given leave to transfer from the regular army and became a lieutenant-colonel in the volunteer Corsican National Guard. After surviving a quarrel with the military authorities

9

in Paris, he was reinstated in the army at the rank of captain. He earned his first major recognition, and in the process sustained the only serious wound of his military career, in the siege of Toulon (December 1793). His impressive performance, helped it must be said by a good deal of luck, earned him immediate promotion to the rank of brigadier-general at the age of twenty-four. Less than two years later he was to make his mark again in the royalist incident of 13 Vendémiaire Year IV (5 October 1795) popularly known as the 'whiff of grapeshot'. Such exemplary use of force both defended the retiring National Convention and dispersed the insurgents, thereby ensuring the Republic's survival under the newly adopted Constitution of the Year III.

The incident is significant not only in terms of Napoleon's career; it also marked the first decisive use of the line army as an instrument of *civilian* repression in Paris since the start of the Revolution, and as such it set a precedent. With the patronage of Paul Barras, one of the first members of the new executive Directory, Napoleon gained command of the Army of Italy in March 1796. The appointment soon enhanced his rising reputation at home and abroad. The first Italian campaign of 1796–7 became legendary for its series of spectacular victories over the Austrians and Piedmontese – at Montenotte, Millesimo, Dego, Ceva, Mondovi, Lodi, Borghetto, Lonato, Castiglione, Roveredo, Bassano, Arcola, and Rivoli, which at last brought the capture of Mantua after an eight-month siege [94, 96]. Napoleon forced the Piedmontese out of the war and then brought the Pope (at Tolentino, 19 February 1797) and soon afterwards the Austrians (at Campo Formio, 17 October 1797) to peace. By that stage he was in effect conducting diplomacy as well as war more or less on his own initiative, without clear reference to or instructions from the Directory, his notional civilian masters.

There were two other important landmarks in Napoleon's career during those dramatic years. First, he married the widowed Josephine de Beauharnais, born Rose Tascher de la Pagerie, in a civil ceremony in March 1796. He was then twenty-six, she thirty-two, with two children by her former marriage. It was something of a 'society alliance', inspired

10

no doubt by her legendary beauty and prominence in the *salons* of the early Directory, and by Napoleon's rising reputation after Vendémiaire. It symbolised the new aura surrounding the best of the career-soldiers borne rapidly aloft by the Revolutionary wars, and demonstrated that the heroic ethic in France under the Directory was essentially a military one. The second development was a further and more serious royalist threat to the Directory on 18 Fructidor Year V (4 September 1797). The attempted coup implicated two directors, Barthélemy and Carnot, as well as Pichegru, the military commander. It was General Augereau, Napoleon's own deputy in Italy, whose intervention proved decisive. The affair was followed by the deportation of its ringleaders, and it marked the last serious royalist challenge to the new political order until 1814. It was another instance of the role of the line army as a major new force in Parisian politics, and after it Brumaire would seem less extraordinary. During the next two years, although Napoleon embarked on his Egyptian campaign (1798–9) [89] and most of his Italian conquests were reversed during his absence, the reputation of the line army as the surest guardian of the republican order held good. With Napoleon's *coup d'état* of 18–19 Brumaire Year VIII (9–10 November 1799) the Directory fell, unpopular and unlamented, a political victim of the new military progeny it had helped to rear.

And so, while the preceding paragraphs have concentrated on Napoleon himself as the most spectacular beneficiary of the changes wrought in the French army by the Revolution, the same process of professional opportunism and advancement might be traced through the military careers of many others. If one looks at the future marshals of the Empire, for instance, one finds that the great majority had been aspiring soldiers in their twenties or thirties at the start of the Revolutionary wars. Some, like Napoleon himself, had had their initial training in the old royal army; others had enlisted in the Republican forces after earlier service in the various contingents of the National Guard. In spite of their professional promise, and with perhaps only a few exceptions, they would surely have lacked the financial means or social connections to rise as fast under the old venal system as they were to do during the Revolutionary wars or later under Napoleon. The ascendant careers of men like Augereau, Bernadotte, Berthier, Bessières, Brune, Davout, Gouvion Saint-Cyr, Lannes, Lefebvre, Macdonald, Marmont, Masséna, Mortier, Murat, Ney, Oudinot, Soult, Suchet and Victor were all part, if at the time a less celebrated part, of the same military dynamic which had brought fame and then power to Napoleon [95].

In 1799 this relatively young constellation of military careerists, not all of whom were open supporters of, let alone participants in the *coup d'état* of Brumaire, were poised for higher honours. Several had already shared the *camaraderie* of service under Napoleon in the first Italian campaign or in Egypt. Yet all, even those who at first had opposed the coup, came to identify themselves with his regime and were in time to benefit from its professional opportunities and social rewards. On a rather less spectacular but certainly much wider scale, one could say the same of the many hundreds of other officers who, rising up the ranks in the 1790s, were to form the top brass of the future Grand Army.

(ii) The evolution of a revolutionary state

France, Napoleon's political inheritance, had also changed in shape and fortune during the 1790s. The first three years of the Revolution, from May 1789 to April 1792, had been a period of peace in France, albeit uneasy towards the end, but one in which the most enduring reforms of the Revolution had been achieved. In the course of those years the National and Legislative Assemblies had abolished the remnants of 'feudalism' in name and to a large extent in practical form as well. Legal distinctions between the three estates or orders of society, the *parlements* and the old judicial system, the administrative divisions of the Bourbon state, venal offices, the tax farms, fiscal privilege, the old *caisses* and their accountants, customs anomalies, craft guilds and trade monopolies – all had been swept away. In their place had come a new system avowedly committed to legal and fiscal equality, new financial institutions, uniform courts for both civil and criminal justice, a reformed framework for departmental and local government, a national customs system, and (exception made for the extraordinary measures adopted during the Terror of 1793–4) the liberation of industry and trade for freer enterprise. The Church had been stripped of its property, nationalised on 2 November 1789, and restructured by the Civil Constitution of the Clergy (12 July 1790). This, in the event, had provoked a profound schism among the clergy and given papal as well as royalist backing to the counter-revolution.

Historians have tried for nearly 200 years to subsume all these reforms under a coherent label. The most familiar is surely still the Marxist idea of a 'bourgeois revolution', marking the Revolutionary decade off from the corrupt and atrophied 'feudal' or 'aristocratic' privileges of the old regime. We know now that this is a simplistic model, that 'feudalism' had lost most of its original meaning in France by 1789, and that commoners had been able to buy their way into privileged status. Moreover, 'capitalism' in the modern sense was then still in its infancy. Its roots and values lay in land, or in what George V. Taylor has called 'proprietary capitalism' [111, 112]. If the French Revolution indeed had a 'bourgeois' theme, it is not to be found in 'modern' industrial, commercial and financial enterprise, which in many ways it actually retarded, but in land. This might also be called proprietary individualism, of which the most important manifestation by 1799 had been the sale of the confiscated Church and émigré property. Some 10 per cent of French land had thus been redistributed with the sale of Church property. The capital value involved has been estimated at around 2000 million livres in terms of the currency of 1790, not counting tithes, which were worth half as much again [76]. In spite of even higher but exaggerated estimates then and since, lands later confiscated from the émigrés, suspects and condemned persons are now thought to have had roughly the same capital value. One should however add that the treasury's actual receipts from the sale of these *biens nationaux* up to 1797 had fallen well short of the notional total of 4 milliard livres, due to the steady

13

depreciation of the paper money [55: *244*]. Moreover, many of the émigré families had proved adept at salvaging what they could from the wreck [116].

By any standards, the sale of such vast resources was a major social and economic development in France during the 1790s. On it, what some historians call 'post-revolutionary society', the society of which Balzac wrote so perceptively in many of his great works, was based. Napoleon had done almost nothing to initiate this process. It was part of his inheritance, and prudently he did not try to meddle with the *fait accompli* of the Revolutionary land settlement. He was to show similar realism in his treatment of the administrative and legal professions, many of whose members had once served the Bourbons and then adjusted their careers to the opportunities of the various Revolutionary assemblies. This is another important link between his inheritance and his own achievements.

Territorially, too, France had changed before Brumaire, and here Napoleon had had at least some influence on the shape of his inheritance. 'Old France', with its 28 million subjects of 1789, had already incorporated the former papal enclaves of Avignon and the Comtat Venaissin (annexed on 14 September 1791), Savoy (27 November 1792), and Nice (31 January 1793). It had also survived threats of foreign invasion in 1792 and again in 1793, before the massive military levies and other emergency measures imposed during the Terror had saved the day. Out of this extraordinary mobilisation of resources had come the momentum for the wars of conquest [23, 92]. As a result of them, the Republican armies had extended French rule over Belgium and Luxemburg (annexed in the form of nine new departments on 30 September 1795), over the German left bank of the Rhine (turned into four new departments in January 1798, though not fully annexed to France until 1801–2), and over Geneva and its environs (one department formed on 26 April 1798) [12]. The Batavian Republic of 1795, successor to the former Dutch Republic of the Seven United Provinces, had been created as a French ally, officially at least, following the Treaty of The Hague imposed on it in May that year [133]. The thirteen cantons

14

of the old Swiss confederation had also been reorganised as the sister Helvetic Republic in May 1798, not least to secure the strategic routes to Italy [137].

Napoleon's campaigns had of course been followed by important constitutional rearrangements in Italy itself, and with the latter he was intimately concerned [141]. The area of Italy conquered first and exposed longest to French rule was Piedmont, taken during the campaigns of 1796–7. However, it remained for the next three or four years torn between French forces battling to maintain their occupation and a royalist counter-revolution led by the successors of Victor Amadeus III, the former king of Sardinia, with Austrian and Russian help. Only after their victory in the Marengo campaign of June 1800 could the French reassert their full hold on Piedmont, and its annexation to France duly followed on 11 September 1802. Meanwhile, the lands of the Republic of Genoa had been reconstituted as the Ligurian Republic in June 1797 and, after its temporary loss to the Austrians in 1799–1800, was also to be reorganised in 1801.

To the east, and north of the River Po, the former Austrian duchy of Milan had passed through its avatar as the Lombard Republic (May 1796), before being renamed the Cisalpine Republic in June 1797. As such, it was at the same time enlarged by the addition of the Cispadane Republic south of the Po (itself formed in the preceding December from the lands of Modena, Reggio, and the papal legations of Ferrara and Bologna) and of Mantua, Romagna, the Valtellina and western Venetia. Soon hailed as a model for others of its kind, it was to become the Republic of Italy in 1801. In due course French intervention had extended to the central and southern parts of the peninsula, although Napoleon had no direct part himself in the creation of the short-lived Roman Republic (1798–9) and Parthenopean Republic centred on Naples (January–June 1799).

Clearly, then, the military thrust of outward expansion, from 'old France' to the so-called 'natural frontiers' of the Pyrenees, the Alps and the Rhine, and even beyond them, had begun *before* Brumaire. Important new resources had been annexed or simply commandeered in the process.

15

By 1800, 'France' consisted of 98 departments, 88 within her metropolitan area, as against the original 83 of 1790. Her population, if Belgium and the German left bank of the Rhine are included, was then around 33 million. Although they were adversely affected by the wars of the 1790s, the Belgian and Rhenish departments were valuable economic accessions. They were among the most industrially advanced parts of continental Europe at that time. Their subsequent economic development under the Consulate and Empire was to demonstrate the rich potential of this particular part of Napoleon's inheritance.

But at what cost had French territorial expansion been achieved before Brumaire? We might consider first the financial difficulties, especially after the hyper-inflation (1795) and subsequent recall (1796) of the assignat, the paper currency of the Revolution [55, 58]. This, among other factors, had necessitated a military policy of 'living off the land' in the conquered territories. The early Girondin rhetoric of 'war on the châteaux, peace for the cottages' (*Guerre aux châteaux! Paix aux chaumières!*) had not in practice turned out so. The reality of the French presence had been encapsulated in the instructions of the Directory to Commissar Joubert in January 1796: 'the principle which contains everything there is to be said on the subject of the occupied territories is: *above all else the army must live*' [119: 59]. Instead of political and economic liberation, the French had brought a persistent despoliation of resources to the conquered areas of Germany and Italy. Furthermore, while the land power of France increased during the Revolutionary wars, her maritime trade was effectively severed by the British navy. Her colonial traffic, which before the Revolution had accounted for roughly a third of her imports and perhaps a quarter of her exports, had withered away [149, 150]. We must recognise the constraints and frustrations of such economic dislocation if we are to understand the purpose of the commercial and industrial policies adopted later during the Empire.

In all, Napoleon's inheritance contained not only expanding assets but some seriously diminishing ones as well. On the one hand, he gained all the human and material resources which the Revolutionary state had mobilised for war. On the other, he faced the disruption caused by French maritime losses and, in Britain, an elusive enemy steadily extending her mastery of the seas. In time, he was to devise extraordinary means in an attempt to bring her down; but in the years immediately following Brumaire the first priority lay in consolidating the bases of his regime in France itself.

3 The Civil Foundations of the Napoleonic State

If the citizens of Paris had become accustomed to the intervention of the line army in civilian politics by 1799, they were probably not aware of just how close Napoleon's *coup d'état* came to being a fiasco. It was a bungled plot, messy and confused, and if it had a true hero, he was Lucien rather than Napoleon Bonaparte. But Lucien, then president of the council of five hundred, having done his work in getting the councils of the Directory dissolved and serving briefly as minister of the interior, was soon packed off to less prominent pastures as ambassador to Spain. Napoleon's propaganda at once presented Brumaire as a resounding personal triumph [46].

Except for the emergency government during the Terror of 1793–4, successive Revolutionary assemblies had sought to decentralise if not executive then at least administrative authority. At the same time their aim had been to vest legislative sovereignty in the central assembly, in other words in themselves, purportedly acting in the name of the people. The Constitution of 1791 had not produced a workable formula for reconciling such legislative authority with the executive functions of the state, and war had soon exposed the weakness. The hamstrung monarchy itself had fallen on 10 August 1792, and on 10 October 1793 the Jacobin Constitution of the preceding June had been officially suspended 'until the peace'. The Directory, for its part, had inherited a much more successful war in November 1795, but had been unable to establish firm political leadership. Its electoral base under the narrow franchise allowed by the Constitution of the Year III

(August 1795) had never been popular. In short, on the eve of Napoleon's coup, Revolutionary France had had three constitutions [41]. All had failed, or could be construed as having failed, to secure effective executive government at the centre and put an end to political factionalism. Brumaire cut short the Directory's unfulfilled experiment with selective republican liberalism by a self-perpetuating propertied élite. Napoleon, with ruthless clarity, saw the need to redeploy and widen that élite, while denying it any real substance of power.

(i) Central, departmental and local government

The Constitution of the Year VIII (13 December 1799) formally established the Consulate and legitimised the *coup d'état* of Brumaire. Officially, it was the work of the three provisional consuls (Bonaparte, Sieyès, Ducos) acting in concert with two legislative committees chosen from the former councils, the five hundred and the ancients, of the Directory. As originally conceived by Sieyès, it had the semblance of internal balance. In the event, however, Napoleon made sure that it was heavily weighted towards the executive authority of the first consul. The latter, appointed in theory by the senate for ten years, was to be assisted by two other consuls, who soon materialised in the persons of Cambacérès and Lebrun.

The constitution became effective on Christmas Day 1799. While affirming the inviolable rights of property and of individual liberty, it avoided any explicit reference to the original Rights of Man and of the Citizen (26 August 1789). Its electoral provisions paid lip-service to the notion of universal manhood suffrage, but in practice annulled any true expression of popular opinion through successive rounds of selection by tenths. This inefficient and often corrupt filtering-up process of communal, departmental and national lists of 'notabilities' favoured propertied men and incumbent officials, many of whom appeared on the lists *ex officio*. An apparently more direct appeal to 'the people' was

19

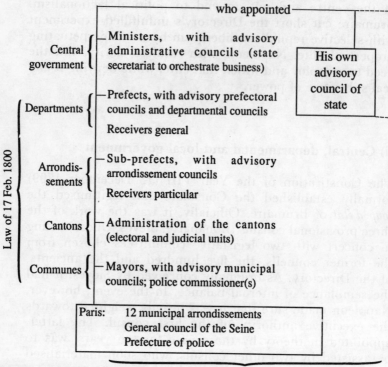

CONSULATE
(Constitution of the
Year VIII/13 Dec. 1799)

EXECUTIVE

Napoleon, first consul

who appointed

Central government { Ministers, with advisory administrative councils (state secretariat to orchestrate business)

His own advisory council of state

Law of 17 Feb. 1800

Departments { Prefects, with advisory prefectoral councils and departmental councils

Receivers general

Arrondissements { Sub-prefects, with advisory arrondissement councils

Receivers particular

Cantons { Administration of the cantons (electoral and judicial units)

Communes { Mayors, with advisory municipal councils; police commissioner(s)

Paris: 12 municipal arrondissements
General council of the Seine
Prefecture of police

LIFE CONSULATE
(Constitution of the Year X/
2 and 4 Aug. 1802)

Napoleon, first consul for life

EMPIRE
(Constitution of the Year XII/
18 May 1804)

Napoleon, hereditary emperor

First abdication (6 Apr. 1814)

Structure of

LEGISLATURE

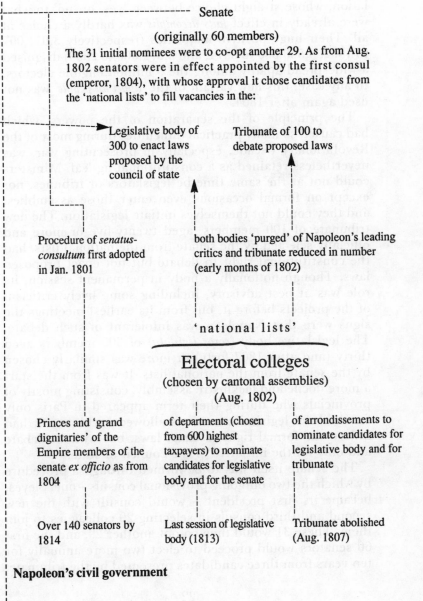

Senate

(originally 60 members)

The 31 initial nominees were to co-opt another 29. As from Aug.
1802 senators were in effect appointed by the first consul
(emperor, 1804), with whose approval it chose candidates from
the 'national lists' to fill vacancies in the:

Legislative body of
300 to enact laws
proposed by the
council of state

Tribunate of 100 to
debate proposed laws

Procedure of *senatus-consultum* first adopted
in Jan. 1801

both bodies 'purged' of Napoleon's leading
critics and tribunate reduced in number
(early months of 1802)

'national lists'

Electoral colleges
(chosen by cantonal assemblies)
(Aug. 1802)

Princes and 'grand
dignitaries' of the
Empire members of the
senate *ex officio* as from
1804

of departments (chosen
from 600 highest
taxpayers) to nominate
candidates for legislative
body and for the senate

of arrondissements to
nominate candidates for
legislative body and for
tribunate

Over 140 senators by
1814

Last session of legislative
body (1813)

Tribunate abolished
(Aug. 1807)

Napoleon's civil government

indeed made in the three plebiscites which confirmed the Constitution of the Year VIII, the life consulate of August 1802, and finally the hereditary Empire of May 1804. But these, especially the first, were exercises in official manipulation, whose straight choice between 'yes' or 'no' to what were already in effect *faits accomplis* was hardly a choice at all. Their huge positive majorities (respectively 3,011,007 to 1562; 3,568,000 to 8374; and 3,572,000 to 2569) disguised a widespread apathy among the 5 million eligible electors. In any case, this new variant of the '*appel au peuple*' was not used again after 1804.

The principle of the separation of the powers, which had caused so many practical difficulties during most of the Revolutionary decade, especially in prosecuting war, was nevertheless retained as a constitutional fig-leaf. Ministers could not at the same time be legislators or tribunes, nor except on formal occasions even enter those assemblies, and they could not themselves initiate legislation. The new tribunate of 100 members, aged twenty-five or more and officially selected by the senate from the national lists, had the constitutional right to debate but not enact proposed laws. Though notionally a body in permanent session, its role was at best advisory, including some lively criticism of the projects before it, but from its earliest meetings the signs were that Napoleon was intolerant of such debate. The legislative body (*corps législatif*) of 300 members aged thirty (and after 1807 forty) or more was similarly chosen by the senate from the national lists. It was from the start a more docile and lacklustre assembly, consisting mostly of provincials who during their term appeared in Paris only for the brief legislative sessions allowed each year. It had indeed the formal right to enact laws, but without debate and only on the initiative of the council of state.

The senate itself was to be formed through a procedure by which the two outgoing provisional consuls – one, Sieyès, became its first president – would consult with the new second and third consuls in selecting 29 colleagues to join them. These 31 would then co-opt another 29, and the first 60 senators would proceed to elect two more annually for ten years from three candidates presented by the tribunate, the legislative body and the first consul respectively, so as eventually to produce a body of 80 strong [38]. In fact, its numbers were to rise above 140 by 1814, since the princes and 'grand dignitaries' of the Empire became members *ex officio* as from 1804, and were reinforced by other later appointments. It was Napoleon's intention that the senators should enjoy more public prestige than the tribunes and legislators. To ensure this, they were to be appointed for life, to receive an annual salary of 25,000 francs each, and were ineligible for any other office of state. They were vested with powers to preserve the constitution, but were also given the right to amend it, on the proposal of the three consuls, by a procedure known as *senatus-consultum*. This procedure, first adopted on 5 January 1801, came to be used more and more to override the wishes of the other bodies [52].

The reforms introduced by the Constitution of the Year X (2 and 4 August 1802) reinforced the filtering-up process in public elections and to it now added an explicitly plutocratic criterion. The new arrondissement and departmental electoral colleges thereby created were to be chosen by cantonal assemblies, but henceforth the members of each departmental electoral college *had* to be among its 600 highest taxpayers (*plus imposés*) and were to serve for life. The first consul was empowered to appoint additional members, who in the case of the departmental colleges were to be selected from the 30 highest taxpayers of the department concerned. He also had the right to appoint the presidents of the cantonal assemblies and of both types of electoral college. Elections to the colleges were to take place once every five years in a stipulated series. At these meetings a specified number of candidates were to be nominated by each department to form composite lists, from which the senate would then elect the legislators and tribunes and also co-opt additional members into its own body [38].

The central advisory and executive organs of state were formed wholly without recourse to such formal electoral procedures. The council of state, whose members were chosen and appointed by the first consul, and who

23

also enjoyed the same salary as senators, was at once an advisory and a supervisory body directly responsible to Napoleon. As such, it was allowed some small margin to influence his will, for instance in drafting the legislation he wished to initiate, and a rather wider one to keep his ministries in check [39]. The latter together formed a central executive to apply rather than question his decisions. They did not in any sense constitute cabinet government, as he dealt with them severally, and there was certainly no suggestion of their collective responsibility.

The key to the management of the civil state lay in the wide purview of the ministry of the interior, whose divisions and bureaux grew like accretions on a coral reef and underwent much internal reorganisation during the Consulate and Empire. Its functions ranged over general and local administration, agriculture and food supplies (*subsistances*), trade, crafts and manufactures (until the end of 1811), public works (including mines, roads and bridges), prisons, public welfare, education, censorship, the arts and sciences, local finances and ministerial accounts, archives, and statistics, the latter becoming progressively more demanding as official inquiries were multiplied in the later years of the Empire [35]. The various *Directions générales* and bureaux set up to deal with all those matters employed a staff almost constantly on the increase, from its low point of 85 under Chaptal (1800–4) to a high of more than 220 under Montalivet (1809–14) [36: *268*].

The ministry of general police was another crucial body [43]. Apart from a period between 1802 and 1804, when it was suppressed and its functions placed under the authority of the ministry of justice, it in many ways symbolised the nature of the regime. After its restoration and reconstitution on 10 July 1804, it kept a close watch on all forms of subversion, real or imagined, and employed a staff of around 120. Consisting of six carefully demarcated sections, and employing a whole network of trained spies, its work is associated above all with Joseph Fouché. A former terrorist and regicide, he was in charge of it from 1799 to 1802 and again from 1804 to 1810, when Savary succeeded him. Its

24

incursions into the underworld of political dissidence and real crime were useful to Napoleon, in spite of the minister's own disloyalty, and its techniques became exemplary as well as notorious [33, 37]. The departments of the expanding Empire were grouped in four large police arrondissements, including that for Paris and another for the area beyond the Alps. All these eyes and ears were supplemented by the Imperial gendarmerie. It was made up of thirty departmental legions, each consisting of two squadrons, and in 1810 counted a total of 18,173 men, of whom 733 were officers [11]. Like some of the enlightened despots before him, Napoleon also appointed secret police to spy on his police. This role fell, among others, to Louis-Nicolas Dubois, the prefect of police in Paris, who in this respect was directly responsible to the emperor and whose prefecture was independent of Fouché's ministry.

Other civil ministries were also reorganised at different times during the period, gaining or giving up certain functions in the process [50]. Each minister had his own advisory administrative council (*conseil d'administration*), and relations between the ministries were orchestrated by a state secretariat, which was itself elevated to ministerial status when the Empire was proclaimed. At its head for most of the period was Maret, through whom the first consul and emperor channelled his instructions to the ministers, and who also had an important say in selecting items to be published in the *Moniteur*. Altogether, the staff of the dozen or so ministries of Napoleon rose from around 1650 at the end of the Directory to more than 2100 under the Consulate, and then, along with their dependent *Directions*, to something between 3600 and 4000 by the late Empire [36: *270*]. Such expansion was due mainly to the growing demands of war.

The recentralisation of executive authority in the first consul and his ministers was in due course extended to the provinces. On 17 February 1800 the Napoleonic prefectures were created in the 98 departments of France [49, 53]. The prefect, appointed by the first consul, was assisted by a number of bureaux at whose head was the general secretary, also appointed centrally, who acted in his absence. He presided over a small prefectoral council and a larger general council, both purely advisory bodies, whose numbers varied according to the population of each department. The first assisted the prefect in settling fiscal, legal, or administrative disputes; the second helped him fix the assessment of direct taxes and of the additional funds (*centimes additionnels*). These councillors were also appointed by the first consul, usually from the lists of departmental 'notabilities', and previous public service or landed wealth played an important part in their selection.

The prefect was in all ways the crucial agent of the central government in provincial France. As one scholar has put it, he was like 'a little emperor' in his department [12: *589*]. Each department moreover was sub-divided into newly formed arrondissements, administered (except in the departmental capital itself) by sub-prefects appointed by the first consul, who in practice often preferred men of moderate political views with local administrative experience. Their functions were wholly subordinated to those of the prefect and consisted mostly of executing his orders, maintaining law and order, assisting in fiscal and military levies, and supervising the business of the municipalities. The arrondissements were in effect enlarged versions of the original districts of 1790, and each had its own advisory council to assist the sub-prefect. Among the first councillors appointed there was again a heavy preponderance of men who had served during the Revolution, along with a smaller representation of wealthy farmers, merchants and manufacturers.

The consular Republic had 402 arrondissements in 1800, and they in turn incorporated a total of 5105 cantons. Under the Constitution of the Year VIII, the latter lost their former administrative functions and were reduced in number and status to electoral and judicial units only. At the same time local government was revived by the restoration of the municipalities, though their number was also reduced. The law of 17 February 1800 provided the definitive structure not only for the larger urban communes of France but also for the small rural ones, of which there were some 40,000. Each commune was to have a mayor, one deputy mayor (*adjoint*) or more to act in his absence, and a municipal council whose membership varied according to its population. A police commissioner was also to be appointed in every commune of between 5000 and 10,000 inhabitants, and more were permitted in the larger towns. Provincial cities exceeding 100,000 inhabitants (Lyons, Marseilles and Bordeaux) were allowed additional mayors and deputies until May 1804, but thereafter Paris alone enjoyed an exceptional status. The appointment of the mayors, deputies and police commissioners widely reinforced the intrusive powers of the head of state.

Taking Napoleon's governmental system as a whole, one is struck by the regularity of its guiding precepts: uniformity throughout, the devolution of administrative authority from the top, a well-ordered hierarchy of status, command and reward within the various professional corps [45, 48]. To achieve this, he laid down firm rules for the training of public officials, most notably by the law of 9 April 1803. Graded scales for salaries and pensions were adopted, and in practice promotion usually depended as much on seniority as merit. Such grading and promotion were strictly applied to new professional groups like the *Auditeurs au Conseil d'état* formed in 1803 [40] and the *Ingénieurs géographes militaires*, while among the lower grades of clerk (*commis*) the range of salaries was wider still [36]. Some critics have noted the frustration caused by lack of promotional opportunities in the higher echelons of the executive, itself an earnest of Napoleon's preference for obedient servants rather than independent initiators. Within the civil state, if not the army, this often acted as a restraint on his celebrated dictum that 'posts will be open to Frenchmen of all opinions, provided that they have the knowledge (*des lumières*), the ability and the qualities (*des vertus*)' – better known in its shorthand form as 'careers open to talents'.

The new incumbents of the high administrative offices reflected all shades of former political opinion, from royalists to regicides and terrorists, whose earlier divisions were

27

now neutralised in obedience to the same master. Relative youth and rapid promotion were also most common among these higher officials. According to Jacques Godechot, no fewer than 79 of the first prefects appointed in March 1800 were forty-three or forty-four years of age [12: *588*]. This is more or less confirmed by Basile Panagiatopoulos, who found that the 'modal year of birth' of the prefects in service in 1806 had been 1758 [47: *444*]. Of the 300 or so who at some time held prefectoral office under Napoleon, furthermore, about 60 had started their careers as auditors in the council of state and were in that sense recently trained professionals.

It should be clear from the foregoing paragraphs that if the Napoleonic administration had a central theme, it was the continuity of personnel across the Brumairean divide. Of the first 300 legislators, for instance, 240 were drawn directly from the councils of the Directory, and of the rest, only 21 had never been members of a previous Revolutionary assembly. More than 200 of the total were in their forties or fifties, and all 300, including even the very few former nobles among them, had shown some public support for the Revolution. Of the first 100 tribunes, whose average age was slightly lower, 69 were former members of the Directorial councils and 5 of earlier assemblies, which left only 26 without such previous experience [38: *19–22*]. Of the first prefectoral appointments, finally, 76 were former members of the various Revolutionary assemblies (15 of the Constituent, 16 of the Legislative, 19 of the Convention, 5 of the council of ancients, and 21 of the council of five hundred). Several had held ministerial or other high executive offices, including the director Le Tourneur. Many more had served in departmental administration or else as mayors of large towns before Brumaire [12: *588*].

(ii) The '*ralliés*' and the opposition

Napoleon's attempt to place himself above what he saw as the destructive factionalism of the Revolution, while neutralising its political impact, became clear early on in carefully measured gestures of appeasement. This marked a break from the Directory's uneasy balancing act between 'left' and 'right', by which it had tipped its weight in whichever direction was required to isolate either Jacobins or royalists, as the occasion had seemed to demand. Napoleon aimed to placate both groups and draw them into a common allegiance to himself, not least by the obligatory oath of loyalty to the Constitution.

Thus on the one hand he allowed the Jacobins who had been deported in the Year III to return to France. On the other, he granted the same concession to former counter-revolutionary groups, first by repealing the law of hostages against the families of royalist émigrés on 13 November 1799, and then by his amnesties to the émigrés themselves on 2 March and 20 October 1800 and on 26 April 1802. Thereafter, the proscribed list was confined to royalists who had held responsible office in the émigré armies, to those whose personal bonds with the exiled Bourbons or their allies were inseparable, and to clerics who refused to accept the Concordat. The great majority of the émigrés returned to France under these amnesties. If not won over to the new regime in an active sense, many of them were at least pacified by the restitution of that part of their confiscated lands which had not been sold off from the national domain, or else by first options of repurchase when their alienated property reappeared on the market [116].

The earliest Napoleonic *'ralliés'* can be identified as those who had furthered their professional careers during the Revolution, often enhancing their social status by the purchase of *biens nationaux*. Three groups were most prominent here: the men of the legal professions, among whom families of the old Robe nobility had some representation; those of the often overlapping bureaucratic services, where again there was a place for former royal *officiers*; and of course the risen generation of career-soldiers, which also included a significant number of the old nobility. Bourgeois careerists were nevertheless preponderant in these major channels of professional and social ascent from the late

29

Directory to the Consulate. If the new regime drew heavily on the Revolutionary personnel in all of them, it did so by confirming in very many cases the appointment of men who were already in office when the Constitution of the Year VIII was proclaimed. Under the system of 'notabilities' introduced by the electoral law of 4 March 1801, incumbent officials were well placed to ingratiate themselves into the favour of the regime, and at the same time jobbed others like them on to the official lists. These scrambling republican careerists became the everyday technicians of Napoleon's civil state [108].

Yet if such links between the consular regime and the Revolutionary past gave a stable base to civil government, they could not themselves guarantee lasting peace abroad or even at home. The rupture of the Peace of Amiens in May 1803 marked the resumption of hostilities which, on land or sea, were to drag on for twelve more years. One easily forgets that the Napoleonic state was by no means altogether secure in the early years. The battle of Marengo (14 June 1800) was by all accounts a close-run thing. Napoleon was not seriously troubled, as the Revolutionary regimes before him so often had been, by widespread unrest among artisans or peasants. Already in abeyance during the late Directory, such urban and rural militancy so far disappeared after Brumaire as to allow him to claim the acquiescence of the popular classes in his regime. Isolated incidents of violent opposition occurred nevertheless, and though summarily dealt with, were reminders of lingering antagonism towards the new order.

The affair of the '*machine infernale*', for instance, the attempted assassination of Napoleon by bomb in the Rue Saint-Nicaise on Christmas Eve 1800, failed by only a few seconds. In fact a plot hatched by implacable royalists, it was twisted into a pretext for the deportation of 130 alleged Jacobins and Babouvists on 5 January 1801. The Cadoudal conspiracy of 1803–4, another royalist plot, was followed by a number of executions, including Georges Cadoudal himself, while Pichegru after his arrest was found strangled in his cell in dubious circumstances. And early in 1804 Napoleon still thought it necessary, for reasons of state, to have the duc d'Enghien, grandson of the prince de Condé and a former commander in the émigré armies, arrested on the foreign soil of Baden. After a summary trial at Vincennes, the captive was executed by firing squad on 20 March 1804.

It was in the early years, too, that liberal opposition to the policies of the new regime expressed itself, most brazenly in the tribunate. Granted this, the years 1802–4 ought to be seen as a time when Napoleon toughened his resolve and widened his authority. The autocratic principle became more pronounced in the civil state when in the early months of 1802 he used the procedures for renewing a fifth of the membership of the legislative body and the tribunate to eliminate the most prominent opposition there. Thus 'purged', both assemblies could more easily acquiesce in the proclamation of his life consulate by the *senatus-consultum* of 4 August 1802, even before the full results of the plebiscite on the issue were known. The same measure also laid down that the tribunate would be reduced to 50 members by the Year XIII and that it would be required forthwith to deliberate in separate sections. Each of these was to be monitored by a section of the council of state, until in August 1807 the tribunate was abolished altogether and its loyal rump transferred to the legislative body [38].

By contrast, the status of the senate was progressively enhanced. The Constitution of the Year X gave Napoleon the power to increase its membership to 120 by new appointments, and in January 1803 he also created the 36 senatoriates (*sénatoreries*), corresponding in area to the assize courts. Each beneficiary was to enjoy an annual income of 25,000 francs in addition to his senatorial stipend, and in recognition of certain judicial and administrative functions in his jurisdiction, also received a stately home there. The Legion of Honour created in May 1802 extended public awards, though on a far smaller individual scale, to a much more numerous category of predominantly military faithful.

The 'purge' of 1802 removed some of the most distinguished of Napoleon's critics from their official arena in the tribunate. Daunou, Benjamin Constant, Ginguené,

31

Ganihl, Thiessé, Thibault, J.-M. Chénier, Chazal and Bara were among those, the so-called 'committee of the Enlightenment in the tribunate', thus eliminated. Their celebrated colleague, the liberal economist J.-B. Say, was soon afterwards listed among the tribunes who would be required to retire in the Year XII. In due course Napoleon turned his wrath on other centres of opposition. The class of moral and political sciences at the Institute, where republican liberals were associated with the diverse group of intellectuals commonly referred to as the 'Ideologues', was suppressed early in 1803. Its members were then redistributed among the second, third and fourth classes of the Institute, and the latter were themselves reorganised to secure closer conformity with the first consul's wishes [51]. Madame de Staël's famous *salon* in the Rue du Bac, which Napoleon on St Helena later described as 'quite an arsenal against me – people went there to be armed knights', was effectively dispersed when in 1803 she was exiled from Paris, and later from France altogether [34, 44].

All this signalled the intensification of what Napoleon once called his 'little war' with the liberal writers of the period. Censorship was increasingly tightened through the press bureau of the ministry of police. By 1810 only four journals still had licences to publish in Paris, the *Moniteur universel* foremost among them. All were mouthpieces of the government, and the single journals then allowed in each department were to be obedient echoes of those central organs [82]. Official propaganda was orchestrated to the themes of Napoleon's Imperial grandeur, most characteristically through elaborate celebration of his military victories. One of its aims was to boost the morale of the 'citizen-soldiers', on whom the regime called repeatedly for valour and sacrifice [83]. Since the state was also the leading patron of the visual arts, its encouragement of grandiose monumentalism, the equation of big with beautiful, left its public stamp on 'Empire style' in painting, architecture and sculpture alike. If the 'unofficial' literature and art of the time were never asphyxiated, they often had to find expression in more circuitous ways at home or abroad. This period marked the cross-roads of Neoclassicism and Romanticism, and for those estranged from Napoleon's favour it proved a troubled passage.

(iii) The financial reforms

Much has been made of the financial mismanagement of successive Revolutionary regimes, and Napoleon's propaganda was the first orchestrated attempt to disseminate that harsh verdict and portray his own achievements as a monument to reason and good order. It is true that the transition from the inflationary paper currency to a new metal coinage had been painful, and that this deflation had produced some classic features of an economic depression in the later 1790s [62]. More serious for the state itself was the chronic shortage of disposable income, since tax collection had fallen notoriously into arrears, and the problem was just as acute at local level. Yet those difficulties had been predictable and, to a large extent, even unavoidable. After the hyper-inflation of the assignat in 1795, also a year of harvest failure and terrible famine in France, *someone* had had to initiate the return to a saner currency. The Directory had begun the unpleasant spadework and had paid the price of growing unpopularity.

Among the early financial reforms of the Consulate was a clearer institutional division between the ministry of finances and the directory, then ministry, of the treasury [60]. Lacking skills and experience in this sphere of government himself, Napoleon called on the services of able and honest men to set his house in order. Gaudin, who in 1799 was appointed to the ministry of finances, the central revenue office, was to hold the post until 1814 and again during the Hundred Days [1, 59]. The treasury, the main expenditure office, was under the charge of Barbé-Marbois from 1801 to 1806. His successor, Mollien, had served since 1800 as director of the sinking fund. His introduction there of double-entry bookkeeping was to be extended to his new office, which he held until 1814 and also during the Hundred Days [4, 7].

Gaudin's major contribution to the new regime was

33

in the reorganisation of tax collection, based on the centralisation of controls and the introduction of a more complete and methodical tax register (*cadastre*) for much of the country. Although the staple direct taxes of the Revolution were kept, their assessment and collection were greatly improved. The land tax (*la foncière*) was of course the principal source of state revenue, and it fell almost entirely on the working agricultural population. But as against the total yield of 240 million francs in 1791, its value in the Year XII (1803–4) had been reduced to 206 million within the area of the 1792 frontiers of France [12: *643*]. Its apportionment at the latter date was also more equitable, thanks to the official cadastral surveys launched during the second half of 1802 and then extended during the following years, notably under Delambre's presidency from September 1807 until the end of the Empire.

Of the other direct taxes carrying over from the Revolution, the most important was that on personal or industrial incomes (*la personnelle-mobilière*) which, in a variety of forms bearing chiefly on the towns, had raised some 60 million francs in 1799. Its yield thereafter tended to fall, not least because of difficulties in defining and collecting it. Following the *arrêtés* of 21 September 1803 and 25 February 1804, it was progressively replaced in Paris and later in other large cities by higher consumer duties (*droits d'octroi*). The smaller taxes on trades and services (*la patente*) and on doors and windows had worked inadequately before Brumaire, and there was little change or improvement in their collection under Napoleon. The last of the 'forced loans' imposed during the Revolution was withdrawn on 18 November 1799 and replaced by the so-called 'additional centimes', charged at the rate of 25 per cent per franc on the land, industrial and personal taxes. They were earmarked mainly for local expenditure and grew steadily in importance.

Altogether, the direct taxes were to yield a fairly steady income of some 250 million francs a year until the military reverses of the late Empire, when their burden had to be sharply increased. In 1813, however, they still made up only 29 per cent of the state's total revenue, not much more than the quarter or so then produced by its combined excise duties on tobacco, alcoholic drinks, and a number of other commodities or services, including (as from 1806) salt, which of course recalled the hated *gabelle* of the old regime [16: *39*]. A central excise office (*Régie des droits réunis*) to control the collection of the newly-named consumer duties on drinks, tobacco, playing cards, public transport, gold and silver ware dated from 1804. In December 1810 the purchase, manufacture and sale of tobacco products were placed under a separate state monopoly. These consumer taxes were supplemented by additional revenue from customs duties, stamp and registry charges.

The incidence and value of all the indirect taxes rose considerably during the Empire, the *droits réunis* alone increasing four-fold between 1806 and 1812, and they were seen more and more as a convenient way of making up shortfalls in the direct taxes. But, even so, the total revenues of the state fell far short of its growing expenses, which increased from some 700 million francs in 1806 to upwards of 1000 million in 1812 and 1813, when military needs accounted for as much as four-fifths of those costs. There were disagreeable implications for the defeated enemies and the subject states of France, whose fiscal potential in war indemnities, confiscations and other levies was siphoned off into a special fund, the *Domaine extraordinaire*. This took distinctive form early in 1810, but its actual yield fell far short of the sums officially demanded [16: *39–40*].

In the Imperial departments themselves, the collection of the direct taxes was entrusted to a whole hierarchy of trained officials. The law of 24 November 1799 did away with the fiscal apparatus of the Directory and set up a new body (*Direction du recouvrement des impositions directes*) in each department. The hierarchy of authority extending from the ministry of finances to departmental and lower functionaries is again very evident here. Inspectors general worked under the direct control of the ministers in Paris. Each department had a receiver general, who had to make monthly payments into a central fund, and each arrondissement a receiver particular.

Major innovations followed the financial crisis of 1805–6, which was itself precipitated by the failure of Ouvrard's speculative venture in search of Spanish American 'piastres' and the subsequent collapse of his commercial group, the *Négociants réunis* [57, 61]. Barbé-Marbois was dismissed as minister of the treasury in January 1806, the convenient scapegoat of the whole affair. Mollien, who succeeded him, was ordered to abandon such unreliable deals with private adventurers and return instead to the original idea of the consular *Caisse de garantie*, which he now elaborated. The law of 16 July 1806 set up the central service fund (*Caisse de service*), into which the receivers general were ordered to pay taxes as they were collected every ten days. In this way the service fund also found the wherewithal to issue bonds in its own name.

The reorganisation of the treasury was equally far-reaching, prompting one financial historian to remark that after Brumaire it was 'turned over to the executive' [56: *230*]. The law of 21 January 1800 suppressed the former treasury commissioners and in their place set up a general directory (*Direction générale du Trésor*) under the authority of the ministry of finances. Before the appointment of Barbé-Marbois as minister of the treasury in 1801, Dufresse had acted as its director general until his death that year. The role of these officials was to ensure the prompt receipt of moneys due and to direct both the transfer and payment of state funds. All payments had to be authorised by an official law or a ministerial mandate. Detailed and certified accounts were required from each ministry, and were to be made public at regular intervals during the Consulate and Empire. In September 1807 a new and more efficient accounts office, the central *Cour des comptes*, was set up to audit state finances and report all cases of default among accountants.

All these reforms in tax collection and public auditing gave a new meaning to the concept of a 'financial year' and enabled the regime to work with something approaching balanced budgets. Public loans or the resort to an over-issue of paper money were thus avoided. Napoleon's own hostility to paper money is well known. He insisted from the start on a sound metal currency, and here he certainly owed something to the reforms of preceding Revolutionary assemblies. On 7 April 1795 the silver franc had replaced the *livre tournois* as the official unit of currency. The assignats themselves had been abolished on 19 February 1796 and, pending their final recall, replaced by the provisional 'territorial mandates'. These measures had not however provided for an adequate stock of new metal coins. At the start of the Consulate, debased coins of earlier issue were still in common circulation, and in the frontier regions foreign money was also used in day-to-day transactions [66].

The basis of the Napoleonic monetary system was laid by the law of 28 March 1803 (7 Germinal Year XI), which thus stamped its mark on what henceforth became known as the '*franc de germinal*' [67]. As a bimetallic standard, it fixed the ratio of gold to silver at 1:15.5. The franc piece was to weigh five grammes of silver, nine-tenths fine, and new coins were to be minted in denominations of one-half, three-quarters, 1, 2 and 5 francs in silver, and of 20 and 40 francs in gold. The issue of pure copper coins in denominations of 2, 3 and 5 centimes was also decreed. In all, this reform was to give France the soundest money in Europe at that time, and it notably strengthened the franc in relation to the pound sterling. Based primarily on a silver standard, it ensured that the circulating medium would have the same value as the unit of account, and it was to remain the foundation of the French currency for well over a century. Attempts were later made to withdraw the debased pieces of earlier issue or, where this was difficult, especially in the annexed territories, to fix their parity more firmly to that of the new coins [68].

Important developments in public banking also dated from the Consulate. The French had been hostile to the idea of a central bank since the collapse of John Law's *Système* in 1720, and the financial upheavals of the Revolution had undermined the state's capacity to initiate any such institution. The formation of the Bank of France on 6 January 1800 was therefore an important innovation, and it came more than a century after the creation of the Bank of England (1694). Its founding capital was 30 million francs, composed of shares of 1000 francs each. On 14 April 1803 it was given a monopoly on the issue of paper notes, two other issuing banks being bought out and subsumed into its operations, which at the same time increased its sharehold capital to 45 million francs. Conceived at first as a private venture which had the support of the government, it counted among its regents and censors most of the outstanding figures of the Parisian banking and merchant élite, from which around 200 of its leading shareholders emanated [63].

After the Bank's serious embarrassment and near collapse during the ructions of the Ouvrard affair, stricter governmental controls were introduced under Crétet, whom Napoleon appointed as its first governor by the reforming law of 22 April 1806 [64]. At the same time its capital was doubled to 90 million francs, but its notes continued to circulate only in large denominations, so that commercial dealings in them were deliberately confined to the financial élite. In practice, then, it operated very largely as the 'Bank of Paris', since the transactions of its branches in Lyons, Rouen and later Lille were relatively insignificant. Nevertheless, it had a major role in establishing the credit of the state and, as such, it also took over some of the functions of other public funds.

Of these latter, the most important was the sinking fund (*Caisse d'amortissement*) set up under Mollien's direction on 27 November 1799. Its original purpose was to assist the treasury in meeting obligations on the public debt, but its functions were later widened to reinforce the credit of the state in other ways. As from 1806 it was allowed to issue its own short-term bonds at 6 to 7 per cent interest. In 1810 it was entrusted with the operations of the *Domaine extraordinaire*, and so also had a hand in the fiscal exploitation of the subject states. In the final years of the Empire it made a large issue of bonds secured only on the anticipated sales of communal property (*biens communaux*). The public response to those sales was poor, however, and the Napoleonic sinking fund ended ironically with the very bogy it had been created to prevent: bonds which had in effect become a disguised form of paper money [16: *46*].

Those were developments of the late Empire in its time of troubles, however, when it was over-extended by military burdens and the additional cost of dynastic grandeur. For most of the earlier period at any rate, the credit of the state in meeting its obligations on salaries and pensions was a distinct improvement on what had gone before under the old monarchy and the Revolution alike. As a result of the financial reforms, government bonds rose appreciably in value from 1799 to 1807, when imminent hostilities in the Iberian peninsula provoked a fall on the market. In view of its public commitment to the prompt payment of annuities and interest in specie, Louis Bergeron has likened the Napoleonic regime to 'a Concordat of *rentiers*' [16: *20*]. On balance, Napoleon dealt effectively with the problem of the public debt, even if in the process he largely repudiated the unpaid debt of the Directory (estimated at 90 million francs) and of Holland (78 million) after its annexation in 1810, and ultimately failed to remedy the mounting deficits on the current account in the years 1812–14. Just as victory in war had helped the Empire to pay its way in the ascendant years, so defeat worsened its insolvency at the end.

(iv) The Concordat and Church–State relations

After the nationalisation and sale of ecclesiastical property, the constitutional church had depended at first on the state for its salaries and upkeep, and in theory its incumbents had owed their cures to direct election by 'active' citizens. These arrangements had never been permanently secured, however, partly because the conflict over the refractory clergy had prolonged the religious schism [76]. In part, those troubles had also stemmed from the decision of 21 February 1795 to uphold the neutrality of the state towards all religious cults but at the same time to deny any of them public funding. Under this policy, or non-policy in effect, an uneasy hiatus had formed from the last months of the Thermidorian Convention through to the Consulate itself [73, 75]. Yet the same law had also encouraged a religious and indeed clerical revival under the Directory, notwithstanding another wave of repressive measures against non-jurors in 1798. This revival was most evident among

Catholic women, and in view of it Olwen Hufton feels able to recount 'how a church was re-established from below long before the Concordat' and how the latter 'represented the recognition of a *fait accompli*' [72: *26*].

Napoleon appears to have had little time for the intrinsic tenets of the Catholic faith himself, but he clearly saw its utility as a social bed-rock and as an ideological anodyne. In 1801, strengthened by victory in the Marengo campaign, he began secret negotiations in Paris with an envoy (Consalvi) of the new pope, Pius VII, who under persistent pressure and renewed military threats eventually agreed to a settlement [80]. The Concordat was concluded on 15 July of the same year but not officially published until Easter Sunday (18 April) 1802, along with an important addendum, the so-called 'Organic Articles'. The latter, which imposed a more obviously caesaro-papist formula on the whole agreement, had been appended without due consultation and immediately offended Pius.

Under the terms of the Concordat, as published, the pope officially recognised the Consulate and thereby sanctioned the *coup d'état* of Brumaire. He accepted Napoleon's insistence that all existing bishops must resign and that their reinstatement and all new appointments must be conditional on an oath of loyalty to the French state. This indeed proved a major obstacle to those recalcitrants who believed that not even the pope might act thus in contravention of the apostolic succession without the authority of the college of bishops, and who now joined the schismatic association known as '*la Petite Église*'. In perhaps his most crucial concession (Article XIII) Pius formally renounced any further claim to the alienated property of the Church. This acceptance of the Revolutionary land settlement was to have enduring effects.

Napoleon, for his part, did not allow the French ecclesiastical hierarchy to enjoy the status of an Established Church, in the sense of exclusive constitutional rights and privileges, as the Anglican Church for instance had been restored in 1660, but officially recognised Roman Catholicism as 'the religion of the vast majority of French citizens'. The structure of the French Church, as it concerned diocesan boundaries and the appointment of archbishops, bishops, and priests, was to be set up in consultation with the Holy See, but under the secular arm of the state. The pope's canonical right of investiture was to be respected, subject to the first consul's prerogative of nomination, as laid down in the 'Organic Articles'. The state undertook to pay all official clerical stipends, which in effect made the French Church a dependency of the lay authority. Under the 'Organic Articles', however, some 80 per cent of the parish clergy were declared removable, and only the *curés* nominated to the chief towns of cantons were to be assured of tenure. All the others (*desservants*) were to serve in subsidiary stations (*succursales*) at the bishops' pleasure. In all cases, non-residence of incumbents was strictly forbidden. Although bishops were allowed to create a cathedral chapter and a seminary in their dioceses, these were not to enjoy any guarantee of state subsidy, and the suppression of the old regular orders during the Revolution was not revoked.

In all, the Concordat was a pragmatic and even 'political' agreement. How far the concordatory church actually matched Napoleon's expectations of it can be traced through the major works of Jean Godel on the diocese of Grenoble (Isère) [69] and of Claude Langlois on that of Vannes (Morbihan) [74]. Godel, in an excellent digest of his principal conclusions, identifies three main 'tensions' at work: that between the French Church and the papacy (gallicanism *v.* ultramontanism), that between bishops and priests (episcopalism *v.* presbyterianism), and that between priests and society (the perception of priestly status by the laity). Napoleon's intention was to reassert that part of the gallican tradition which upheld the regulatory rights of the state, but to eliminate all traces of the presbyterian principle associated earlier with Jansenist reformers acting in the frequent absences of many bishops from their dioceses. He similarly wished to re-establish the episcopal tradition of clerical authority from the top, but to detach it from old ultramontane loyalties. And, by turning bishops and priests into something like salaried administrative servants, he aimed to assimilate them to the professional and territorial structures of the lay state. Bishops were thus to be regarded

41

as 'prefects in purple' (albeit on only a third of the pay) and the tenured *curés* as 'mayors in black', all working closely with their civil homologues [70].

In the event, as Godel goes on to show, the Concordat produced some paradoxes quite at variance with Napoleon's intentions. By involving Pius VII in the agreement officially and irreversibly, he had made it impossible for the concordatory church to work smoothly without the pope's continued blessing. By securing the subservience of the bishops to the state, and the subservience of the priests to their bishops, he had resurrected a clerical hierarchy which in the long run would direct its first obedience towards Rome. 'Napoleon wanted a gallican church and obtained an ultramontane church, not only because he did not perceive the evolution which had started, but also because he made it easier' [70: *844*]. If the immediate secular master should falter or fall, the subservience required of his episcopate might be transferred instead to the spiritual authority. The obedience of French bishops to the Holy See later in the century was to make that scenario only too real.

Such conflicting loyalties indeed led to serious ruptures even before the fall of the Empire. Cardinal Caprara, the papal legate in Paris, was unable to prevent a breach in Church–State relations in 1808, when he was recalled. Pius VII would not agree to Napoleon's divorce from Josephine, having remarried them according to Roman Catholic rites at the time of the Imperial coronation. The application of the Continental Blockade, which was among the factors prompting the French military occupation (1808) and annexation (1809) of the Papal States, widened the rift. When in 1809 Pius excommunicated Napoleon and refused to invest any of his nominees to bishoprics, the emperor reacted by imprisoning him, first at Savona (1809–12) and then in much harsher circumstances at Fontainebleau (1812–14) [71]. In 1811 he also summoned a national council of bishops to approve his resolution that, in the event of papal refusal, the canonical right of investiture might be exercised by French metropolitans; but to his intense annoyance the council obeyed the pope on the issue.

Moreover, in spite of its specious incentives to clerical careerism, the Concordat did not significantly boost recruitment into the priesthood. Complaints by the clergy about their inadequate funding, as well as disputes over the management of church 'fabrics', were constant professional frustrations. Potential ordinands were also excluded by the state's insistence on an age qualification and by their liability to military conscription. Between 1802 and 1814 there were only 6000 new ordinations in France as a whole, rather fewer than the deaths among priests during the same period, and not much more than the *annual* average number at the end of the old regime. As against the 60,000 seculars and 70,000 regulars of 1789, there were barely 36,000 seculars in 1814 [16: *193*]. As a result, the incumbent clergy tended to become a noticeably ageing group. Even in areas where there was no apparent crisis of ordinations, new recruits were predominantly of peasant stock. Langlois speaks of the 'ruralisation' of the clergy in his exemplary Breton diocese, a process whose roots probably lay well back in the old regime, and contrasts it with the anticlericalism or religious indifference of the urban classes [74]. In fact, the concordatory church was essentially a *rural* church and, as Lamennais observed so presciently in his *Réflexions sur l'état de l'Église en France* (1808), was long to remain so.

What, then, did the Concordat positively achieve for the Napoleonic regime? Coming as it did around the time of the Peace of Amiens, it certainly played its part in reconciling the mass of the French people with the consular regime and later in sanctioning the hereditary Empire. It further helped Napoleon's pacification of the Vendée (Treaty of Beauregard, 12 February 1800), where sporadic insurgence had continued after the major defeat of the counter-revolutionary rebellion in 1793. It marked a reconciliation with the earlier refractory church and, by thus undermining the old bonds between non-jurors and émigrés, it was a serious blow to royalist exiles. It officially ended the schism provoked by the Civil Constitution of the Clergy in providing a basis for willing non-jurors and jurors to sink their differences in a common service. The 'Organic Articles' furthermore allowed other religions to be legally practised. Napoleon consolidated this policy by separate agreements with French Protestants, both Calvinists (who then numbered nearly half a million) and Lutherans (some 200,000), whose pastors also became salaried servants of the state as from 1804 [78]. Later agreements with the Jewish communities extended his official control over the religious organisation of France [77, 79]. If the Jews were often still the victims of popular hostility and actual social disabilities, many wealthy Protestants came to play a prominent part in the public life of the Empire, and not only in the financial world which they had long since penetrated.

(v) Justice, the Napoleonic codes, and education

The institutional and regional anomalies which had characterised the legal patchwork of the old regime had been rationalised by the Revolutionary reforms [12]. The legal system which Napoleon inherited was not changed fundamentally, in spite of its new nomenclature, but there was a good deal of scope for its reorganisation. Napoleon's 'fundamental principle', J.M. McManners has commented, 'was the soldier's hatred of disorder' – and in that sense he regarded his system of justice as a crucial safeguard of public order [26]. It also became a key element of his administrative uniformity [81, 84].

For *administrative* it indeed was in large part. Above the level of the justices of the peace, judges were appointed for life and in theory enjoyed independence of conscience, but they also owed their selection and the advancement of their careers to the state. The courts of first instance were situated in the chief towns of each arrondissement to apply both correctional and civil justice. As from the Year IX they worked in association with deputies of the commissioners appointed by the central government to initiate prosecutions in the departmental criminal tribunals, or *cours d'assises* as they later became. These were supplemented by the departmental civil tribunals. The location of the appeal tribunals, or *cours d'appel* as from 1804, recalled the appellate system of the old regime. On average, each of them had

44

jurisdiction over four departments, and in April 1810 they were renamed 'Imperial courts'. There were in addition a number of independent special tribunals, like those for trade (*tribunaux de commerce*), which did not find favour with liberal critics of the regime.

Among the most important and enduring reforms of Napoleon were the legal codes, of which the Civil Code (*Code civil des Français*) of 21 March 1804 soon gained a monumental status. In 1807 it became the *Code Napoléon* and, officially at any rate, was implemented in all the subject states, as well as in the French dependencies overseas after 1815. And yet its 2281 articles were not so much major innovations as a grand recapitulation of no less than thirty-six laws passed severally between 1801 and 1803. It was the collaborative work of a commission of four, at whose sessions Napoleon had frequently presided, personally supervising the drafts, so that his own conservative values, instinctively felt, could be translated into more refined legal form. Its three sections deal with the rights of persons, of property, and of the acquisition of property. Among its most crucial provisions, at least for the beneficiaries concerned, were those giving fixed legal title to the earlier sales of confiscated Church and émigré property. With some modifications, it also reaffirmed the Revolutionary principle of *partage*, that is the division of estates among all the male heirs in place of the old rights of primogeniture.

All this, in effect, was to sanction some of the most important social developments of the 1790s, but on many other points the legislative reforms of the Revolution were diluted or abandoned. While the principle of legal equality was formally upheld, the details of the Civil Code spelt out the terms of a rather more distributive justice. The paternalistic ethic, for instance, gave heads of families full legal rights over their children. Wives were made legally subservient to their husbands, notably in rights of divorce and in the inheritance of property. Taken as a whole, the Civil Code formalised the reign of order, of uniformity, and of authority from the top. Anticipated in part by the land laws and other judicial reforms of the

45

Revolution, it unequivocally reformulated them to suit the guiding precepts of the Napoleonic state [86].

The process did not end there, for in due course the whole corpus of French law was to be codified in a way never before attempted. By the time the Empire reached its height, the Code of Civil Procedure (1806), the Commercial Code (1807), the Criminal Code and Code of Criminal Procedure (1808), and the Penal Code (1810) had also been promulgated. The Rural Code, which had been debated for many years before Brumaire, made some headway too, but given the great regional diversity of France it proved an altogether more elusive chimera. It was never implemented in fact, and its complexities continued to frustrate all subsequent regimes.

State control and official propaganda were much more obvious in educational policy, where the regime could exploit the natural instincts of careerism among teachers, and where some of the innovations were again to prove remarkably enduring. Public literacy itself was not markedly improved; Napoleon's achievement lay more in the reorganisation of structures and talents within the existing élites. His emphasis was on loyalty and public service in the furtherance of his own grandeur, most evident perhaps in the Imperial Catechism introduced into all state schools as from 1806.

State provision for the education of the general public had been virtually unknown under the old regime. An attempt at standardisation had been made during the Revolution through the *écoles centrales*, but like other civil institutions they had suffered from lack of political will and from inadequate funding under the Directory, and by Brumaire had had little general impact. Napoleon's educational reforms followed the same principle of centralisation but proved institutionally much more effective, mainly because his view of education was essentially functional. As such, he closely related it to the practical needs of the state and to the professional prospects of his educators. The main aim was to train the future military and civil leaders of France. He paid little attention to the elementary schools and largely neglected the education of women. Technical training, by contrast, was encouraged in a number of ways: a Conservatory for Arts and Trades in Paris, smaller trade schools in some provincial towns, and of course the reconstituted Polytechnic. Founded in 1794, the latter fed the special schools and through them the technical services of the state, especially on the military side [85].

The regular schools were set up according to the law of 1 May 1802. Based on Fourcroy's recommendations, it reorganised primary and more particularly secondary education under a directory of public instruction, headed by a councillor of state in the ministry of the interior. Its major innovation was the *lycées* in place of the *écoles centrales*. Each court of appeal was to have at least one of the new schools, whose instructors Napoleon was to choose himself. Of the 6400 state scholarships provided for at these *lycées*, over a third (2400) were reserved for the sons of soldiers and civil officials. In 1808 the *agrégation* was reinstated as a qualification for the recruitment of teachers. As from 1809 the curriculum, based on Latin and mathematics sections, was standardised by the introduction of the baccalaureate examination. Strict governmental supervision, at times almost akin to military precision, was imposed on this system from the start. The communal and private schools were also brought under the control of the prefects. Administrative councils were introduced into all private secondary schools in October 1803, which had an important bearing on the choice of teachers, and the influence of the clergy on private education was further restrained by several measures in 1811. For all that, clerical participation in teaching and in educational administration revived under the Empire, in public as well as private schools. Outwardly at least, it served the interests of the state and was consistent with the Concordat.

The same principle of centralised control and standardisation was extended to the higher echelons of education, for instance at the École Normale Supérieure in Paris, which dated from the Revolution. The so-called 'Imperial University' first took theoretical shape as the 'University of France' in the law of 10 May 1806, but its practical formation came only after the enabling decree of 17 March

47

1808. In effect an agglomeration of bodies, more a teaching corporation than a university, it also bore the influence of Fourcroy's ideas. Its monopoly of public education beyond secondary level was upheld, officially at least, and it enjoyed a generous annual subsidy from the state. Louis de Fontanes, the friend of Chateaubriand and in other ways sympathetic to Catholics, became its first grand master, and was assisted by a chancellor and a council. As such, he was placed directly under the emperor's authority. If in some ways he often circumvented that authority, in others he transmitted it through a hierarchy of officials in the twenty-seven provincial 'academies' and lower down in the local schools which collectively formed the Imperial University [45].

(vi) Summary

In all, the civil foundations of the Napoleonic state supported a massive superstructure held together by the overriding force of autocratic rule. Its ramifications extended into the administrative, economic and social life of all departments. At the centre, Napoleon had turned the major organs of state to his will and dominated them directly. In the provinces, that same will passed down the hierarchy from prefects to sub-prefects and mayors, from police commissioners to small local constabularies, from receivers general and receivers particular to petty municipal tax collectors, from an ecclesiastical establishment of bishops to tenured *curés* and so on to their various parochial subordinates, from higher to middle and lower incumbents of the judicial and educational services alike.

The binding themes of this great work of reconstruction lay, essentially, in the elaboration of authority from the centre and from the top, in the continuity of recruitment and advancement of officials across successive constitutional changes, and in the professionalisation of public functions. In that sense, to quote from Harold T. Parker's recent statement, 'Napoleon as administrator may be termed the originator of modern centralized bureaucracy in France', carrying to fruition 'the long struggle of the French kings to bring their subjects under the administrative control of the central government' [10: *8*]. The factionalism of earlier Revolutionary regimes was neutralised by the concentration of power in a head of state who demanded one common loyalty, and who himself chose and appointed his top officials at every level.

Service in the Napoleonic civil state was open to experienced administrators of all former political affiliations, so long as they accepted the new rules of obedience, that is of subservience. This has sometimes been called a policy of 'assimilation' or of 'amalgamation'. It has also been characterised as a system of 'careers open to talents'. Such descriptions stand up if one compares the professional recruitment of the Consulate and Empire with that of the old regime and even with that of the Revolutionary assemblies, although it must be said that the latter had already prepared much of the ground in sweeping away the hereditary and venal privileges of the Bourbon state. At the same time Napoleon's system could scarcely be likened to a modern competitive 'meritocracy'. In his civil appointments he generally put greater store by seniority and personal loyalty than by merit alone, while his own procedures for the training of young administrators and instructors were by no means free of personal favouritism.

Furthermore, the emphasis of Napoleon's professional selection and promotions itself changed over the years 1799–1814, evolving with his own ambition and pursuit of Imperial grandeur. The relative 'democracy' of republican careerists under the early Consulate gradually gave way to a system more grandiose and even 'aristocratic' in social design during the Empire. In many ways, too, Napoleon's civil state absorbed and exuded the military ethos of its commanding war-lord, with its graded ranks of authority and obedience, its codes of quasi-martial discipline, and its elaboration of an essentially personalised heroic ethic. Behind the civil state, and reinforcing it at every point, stood the army. This interplay of civil and military functions was crucial throughout the period, and to its wider territorial and military extensions we should now turn.

4 The 'Grand Empire' and the 'Grand Army'

On 18 May 1804 the republican Consulate ended with the proclamation of the hereditary Empire, an act solemnised at Napoleon's coronation in the following December. The Empire then consisted of 108 departments, six in Piedmont (later reduced to five) and four on the German left bank of the Rhine having been added in 1802 to the 98 of 1800. On 30 June 1805 it was also to incorporate the reconstituted Ligurian Republic, along with its vital port of Genoa, which now formed three new departments. The new edifice was a military quite as much as a civil establishment. The Grand Army indeed was to have a crucial role in furthering Napoleon's continental power during the years 1804–11. The official shape of his Empire was pushed outwards into areas which lay well beyond the old notion of the 'natural frontiers' or *grandes limites* of France. Early in 1811 the 'Grand Empire' reached its maximum territorial extent.

(i) Territorial and dynastic aggrandisement

The first stage in this process of Imperial aggrandisement involved the defeat and reduction of Austrian power during the course of 1805. By the French victories at Ulm (20 October) and Austerlitz (2 December), and by the ensuing Treaty of Pressburg (26 December), Napoleon had cleared the way for his major reconstruction of Italy [129]. He had already converted the Republic of Italy into a kingdom (March 1805), centred on Lombardy, soon afterwards

50

assuming the crown himself but entrusting its government to his stepson, Eugène de Beauharnais, as his viceroy. Its territory was expanded by the inclusion of Venetia in 1806 and of the Papal States of Urbino, Macerata, Ancona and Camerino in 1808. When Austria was again defeated at Wagram (5–6 July 1809), the Trentino and south Tyrol were ceded to the kingdom by the ensuing Treaty of Schönbrunn (14 October). In March 1806 a new satellite kingdom of Naples was also formed from the lands of the Spanish Bourbons on the mainland, with Joseph Bonaparte as its monarch, although Sicily remained under Anglo–Bourbon control. In May 1808 Parma and the kingdom of Etruria, the latter a Spanish secundogeniture since 1801, were reorganised into four new departments and annexed to the Empire. This offended Tuscan patriots, and in the following year Napoleon made a formal gesture of appeasement by creating the grand duchy of Tuscany, which he entrusted to his sister Élisa and her husband, Prince Bacciochi, though its lands were to remain an integral part of the Empire. What was left of the Papal States, first occupied in February 1808, was formally annexed on 17 May 1809, and on 17 February 1810 Rome itself became 'the second city of the Empire'.

In May 1806 the Batavian Commonwealth came to an end. Its lands were turned into the new kingdom of Holland, to whose throne Louis Bonaparte was appointed in June of that year [133]. Earlier still, during the course of 1803, Napoleon had reorganised the Swiss Confederation and been named as its 'Mediator' [137]. The defeat of Prussia in the twin battles of Jena and Auerstädt (14 October 1806) removed the remaining German threat to Napoleon's new satellite grouping, the Confederation of the Rhine, formed by a constitutional act of 12 July 1806, with the emperor himself as its 'Protector'. Extending the process of 'mediatisation' which had begun at the 'recess' of the German diet in February 1803, this was the immediate cue for the abolition of the Holy Roman Empire, the historic *Reich*, which duly followed in August 1806. The Confederation consisted initially of sixteen signatories but later incorporated several other states, of which the most

51

important were the newly formed kingdoms of Saxony (December 1806) and of Westphalia (July 1807). The youngest of Napoleon's brothers, Jérôme, was appointed as ruler of the latter, formed from the lands of Hesse-Cassel, Brunswick, Wolfenbüttel, Prussian territory west of the Elbe, southern Hanover, and some smaller secular and ecclesiastical principalities. In November 1807 it was given a much-vaunted 'model' constitution [118].

The Fourth Coalition raised by the Allies against Napoleon finally collapsed in 1807 when Russia was defeated at Eylau (7–8 January) and at Friedland (14 June). By the Treaty of Tilsit on 7 July that year Alexander I agreed to apply Napoleon's recently proclaimed 'Continental Blockade' of British trade in the Russian ports and recognised French territorial acquisitions and constitutional innovations in Italy and Germany. Prussia, the subject of a punitive treaty at Tilsit two days later, was deprived of roughly half her former territory and saddled with a war indemnity equivalent to 311 million francs, to be paid in specie. If the kingdom of Westphalia was to be the buttress of the Tilsit agreements in the west, Napoleon's eastern buffer was the new duchy of Warsaw, carved out of the conquered Polish lands on 22 July 1807 and entrusted to his ally Frederick Augustus, the king of Saxony.

Napoleon also intervened directly in the affairs of the Iberian peninsula and of the Adriatic hinterland. In June–July 1808, following the special meeting of a Spanish National Assembly summoned by Napoleon to Bayonne, whose members had been hand-picked to serve his interests, a new satellite kingdom of Spain was created [131]. To replace the deposed Bourbon monarchs, Charles IV and his son Ferdinand VII, Joseph Bonaparte was transferred from Naples to be its ruler [121], being succeeded there by Murat, the husband of Caroline Bonaparte and formerly the grand duke of Berg. Meanwhile, Junot had subjugated Portugal at the end of 1807 and been appointed its governor general in February 1808, while the house of Braganza fled to Brazil. In 1809, after the Austrian defeat, Dalmatia, Istria and part of Carniola and Carinthia became the so-called 'Illyrian Provinces' of the Empire.

If we discount Napoleon's erratic fortunes during the Peninsular War of 1807–14 and his ill-fated Russian campaign of 1812, the last phase of the outward expansion of his 'Grand Empire' came in 1810–11, when he tightened his military, political and economic grip on northern Europe. Early in 1810 the remaining parts of Hanover, occupied by the French since 1804, were formally ceded to the kingdom of Westphalia, although in the following December its richest lands were to be detached and turned over to Napoleon's *Domaine extraordinaire*. In April 1810 Cisrhenan Holland was formed into two departments and directly annexed to the Empire. In July 1810 the rest of Holland followed suit, and in the following December and January the Hanse towns (Hamburg, Bremen, Lübeck) and the grand duchy of Oldenburg were also annexed. French influence north of the Baltic had already been enhanced by the appointment of a Napoleonic marshal, Bernadotte, as Crown Prince of Sweden, heir to the childless Charles XIII, on 21 October 1810.

In addition to his territorial acquisitions Napoleon gained new dynastic recognition by his marriage to Marie-Louise of Austria on 2 April 1810 and by his urgent fathering of an heir, the 'King of Rome', born on 20 March 1811. The Habsburg Emperor, Francis I, was at last a formal ally and was then represented in Paris by the considerable voice of Count Metternich, the go-between of the marriage alliance. The official frontiers of the French Empire at its height in 1811 contained 130 departments with a total population of some 44 million. The 'Grand Empire' reached out further to include satellite kingdoms in Italy, Spain and Germany, many other confederate states on the Rhenish right bank and in Switzerland, the core of Poland, and the north-eastern littoral of the Adriatic. In all, it counted more than 80 million subjects, although a good many in the Iberian peninsula were openly rebellious. Ironically, it was at just this point of supreme territorial and dynastic grandeur that the economic base of the Empire began to weaken, following the crisis of 1810–11, as we shall see in a later chapter.

One might ask, finally, how far the steady growth of

Imperial power in the years 1804–11 was the systematic working out of a master-plan present in Napoleon's ambition from the start. That he assumed power with a 'grand design' seems clear, but the evidence also suggests that it was an evolving rather than a fixed and predetermined one, an ambition which was itself inflated by the military dynamic of successive conquests. In this sense one may say that Napoleon, the realist, forged his 'Grand Empire' by pragmatic opportunism, step by step, working from the military preliminaries to the dynastic and political embellishments. What is not in doubt is that the Grand Army was the crucial instrument of French aggrandisement and that the victories of 1805–7 opened the way to a continental empire which had not been practicable before. We need, then, to understand the underlying military structures which formed the hard base of Napoleon's power.

(ii) The military establishment

In one respect the Napoleonic state marked a major break from the Revolutionary past and indeed from the old regime. Napoleon was at the same time head of state and active commander-in-chief of the army, in spite of his initial lip-service to the Republican principle of separating the two offices. His regime therefore combined its supreme civilian and military functions in his own person. Disputes between the two did not arise, as hitherto they so often had, and this had a crucial bearing on the mobilisation of resources and on the whole ethos of the civil establishment.

At central level, first, there was the ministry of war. Before Brumaire, it had already undergone several reorganisations, but its most important reform came in 1802, when it was divided into a ministry of war and a ministry of war administration (*Administration de la Guerre*). To the older 'core' ministry Napoleon entrusted the management of the combat forces: conscription, promotions, salaries and pensions, troop movements, artillery operations, and the like. From 1800 to 1806 it was headed by Berthier, a veteran of the American campaigns and also Napoleon's chief of staff. His successors there were Clarke (1807–14) and, during the Hundred Days, Davout. The new ministry took over the main commissariat role of providing food and clothing as well as the organisation of military transports and hospitals. It was headed in turn by Dejean (1802–9), Lacuée de Cessac (1809–13), and Daru (1813–14, 1815). The council of state itself included a special war section in which Napoleon's say was intrusive and altogether the decisive factor. Before the division of 1802, the ministry of war had had nearly 500 employees; by 1814 the two ministries had a combined staff of some 1500, a very much higher number than any other [36: *270, 374*]. They drew on the expertise of several specialised services. Daru, for instance, before his appointment, had served as intendant-general of the Grand Army and also of the conquered territories, notably in and after the campaigns of 1805–7 [88]. In that capacity his fiscal functions were supplemented by those of François Roullet de la Bouillerie, the receiver-general of the Grand Army and after 1810 also treasurer-general of the *Domaine extraordinaire*.

France had been organised into 23 military divisions in 1791, each centred on a major town (*chef-lieu de division*). As the territory of the Empire was extended under Napoleon, so these divisions increased to 32 by 1811, including those in Belgium, the Rhenish left bank, Piedmont, Liguria, Tuscany, Rome, Holland, and Hamburg, and there were then six more in the Kingdom of Italy. The size of each division varied according to the importance of the area. Paris, for example, which had a military governor (Murat) from early in 1804, was the seat of the first division grouping the departments of the Seine, Seine-et-Oise, Aisne, Seine-et-Marne, Oise, Loiret, and Eure-et-Loir. Other divisions, again, covered as few as three departments. The respective military divisions were placed under the authority of divisional generals, who had resident commandants and adjutants under their orders [11].

The theme of professional advancement and social ascent from the Revolution to the Empire was if anything more dominant among the officer corps of the army than in the civil establishment. The original marshals appointed on 19 May 1804, at the Empire's inauguration, four with honorary status and fourteen on the active list, offer a selective social physiognomy of the risen warrior class. All the honorary marshals had already been elevated to the senate. At least five of the eighteen (Berthier, Davout, Kellermann, Pérignon, Sérurier) could claim old noble antecedents of some sort. By contrast, five others (Augereau, Lefebvre, Lannes, Murat, Ney) had a family background in humble trades that might justify the description 'working class'. The rest were of various bourgeois stock, whether in the legal profession (Bernadotte, Brune, Moncey, Soult), in the trades (Masséna and Mortier), or in medicine (Bessières and Jourdan, both sons of surgeons). The eight marshals subsequently appointed reflected the same range of social backgrounds. Marmont was of petty noble origin; Poniatowski, the only foreigner so honoured by Napoleon, was a Polish prince, though he died in the battle of Leipzig only two days after his elevation to the marshalate; and Grouchy hailed from an old family of the Sword nobility. Suchet was the son of a silk manufacturer, but the others had humbler roots: Victor (law), Macdonald (the army, the descendant of a Scottish émigré), Oudinot (brewing), and Gouvion Saint-Cyr (tanning) [95].

On a much wider scale, the pioneering work of Georges Six more than forty years ago published important findings on the professional and social composition of the higher officer corps under the Revolution and Napoleon [103]. Taking as his total sample the 2248 generals who held commissions at some time between 20 April 1792 and 5 April 1814, Six found that more than half (1243) had started their careers in the old royal army and never joined a volunteer corps during the Revolution. Another 477 had served in the royal army, or else in foreign armies before the Revolution, and then also in the various volunteer units; but only 337 (some 15 per cent) were volunteers in the strict sense. Of the original total, moreover, 632 generals (just over 28 per cent) were former nobles of the old regime, including 214 titled nobles. The proportion rose to 30 per cent during the later Directory, but had fallen back to 20 per cent by the end of the Empire. Most commonly, the officers in question had originated from the ranks of non-titled military families (*écuyers*). Of the rest, if one excludes the 100 whose social background is obscure, at least 1516 generals must therefore have been of commoner origin. They included 87 who were the sons of manual workers or domestic servants, and 90 others who were the sons of *cultivateurs*, that is of working but by no means always poor peasant stock.

When confining his sample to the Empire itself, Six found that between 25 March 1804 and 3 April 1814 the high command included 174 generals who had served as such before the Revolution, during the wars of the 1790s and then of the Consulate, and whose noble status dated from before 1789. The figure was made up of 5 foreign princes, 8 marquises, 30 counts, 2 viscounts, 8 barons, and 121 *écuyers*. In addition, 131 nobles of the old regime (7 marquises, 22 counts, 6 viscounts, 2 barons, and 94 *écuyers*) had been promoted to the rank of general during the Revolution and thereafter also served as such at some time in the Imperial army [103: *28–9*]. On this evidence, at least 305 of the generals serving at some stage under the Empire could claim nobility of the old regime, among them 90 from titled families, not to mention the generals whom Napoleon himself ennobled. Since these 305 formed a larger group than the generals of humble working-class families, it follows that the vast majority of Napoleon's generals must have been of various bourgeois origin. The process of social assimilation under a common loyalty is again evident here; so is the accompanying theme of pragmatic realignment among the professional officers. The result was a new breed of military *notables* who counted among Napoleon's functioning élite.

Something of the same pattern emerges from Jean-Paul Bertaud's sample study of the much more numerous company-grade officers. Restricting his analysis to 480 captains, lieutenants and sub-lieutenants appointed in or after 1800 and still serving in 1814, admittedly only a small fraction of the total, Bertaud found that just under 5 per cent were of the old nobility, while another 0.5 per cent were nobles of the Empire. The sons of commoner-landowners made up the largest category (22.1 per cent). All the rest hailed from various bourgeois or humbler rural backgrounds, as the following percentages show: *rentiers* (9.6), *cultivateurs* (9.3), lesser merchants and tradesmen (8.7), lawyers (8.4), military families (7.2), artisans (7.2), commercial businessmen (6.9), manufacturers (4.9), administrative functionaries (4.6), professors, teachers and engineers (3.2), day labourers (0.5), and others (0.2) [91: *104*].

In that same article Bertaud also explains what Napoleon expected of his officers and the criteria for their promotion. He had inherited from the Revolution three main principles here: merit, talent, and elections. In the event he accepted but also adapted the first two, while doing away with the third altogether. By his decision of 1805 on officer promotions he kept the nomination of generals and corps leaders to himself; and although he allowed the commanding colonels to propose two-thirds of the nominees to company-grade rank, subject to his approval, he again insisted on nominating the remaining third himself. The requirements for all such promotions were established as length of previous service, the period of service in existing ranks, and evidence of bravery. He believed, as Bertaud puts it, 'that this scouting for talent could only be achieved among the higher ranks of society – those who, thanks to their birth or fortune, were fit to give or receive schooling' [91: *94*].

The officer corps of the Grand Army thus became a microcosm of Napoleon's plans for society at large: to blend the old nobility with the bourgeoisie of talent into a new class of Imperial *notables*. His vision combined an old honorific ethic with a newer plutocratic principle as important criteria of selection, and the army was to be a showpiece of this process of assimilation. Its status as a functioning élite was officially elevated, again within a hierarchy of ranks, by his system of rewards. This in turn raises the question of how far in that process earlier martial values were changed, and possibly even distorted, or how far the concept of 'Honour' during the Empire differed from the Revolutionary ethic of 'Virtue' as the principal motivation of aspiring officers.

Now, in a provocative essay John A. Lynn has recently

argued that there was a 'moral evolution' in French military motivation from the wars of the Revolution to those of the Empire [99]. He sees a transition from an 'Army of Virtue' at the height of the Terror, responsive to the patriotic and if necessary sacrificial call of republican principles, towards an 'Army of Honor' under Napoleon, more responsive to personal reward for service and to associated glory within a quasi-monarchical code of values. The controversy aroused seems already to turn chiefly on an acceptable definition of 'Virtue' in the 1790s and on Lynn's apparent confusion of 'Honour' (in a value-based sense) with 'honours' (in the sense of rewards, or 'baubles' as Napoleon himself once called them). It is unlikely that all Republican officers fought disinterestedly for virtuous causes. Apart from the natural instincts of careerism, the predatory conduct of so many of them in the occupied territories during the Directory suggests rather more material incentives. And it would be equally misleading to imply that 'Honour' (or 'honours' for that matter) was incompatible with a moral sense of patriotic service and sacrifice in Napoleon's armies.

The real motivation of officers on active service will probably not be gauged from the fine words of ideologues, politicians for the most part, presuming to speak in their name. In any event it is clear that much greater emphasis was placed under the Empire than during the Revolutionary wars on the *ceremonial* functions of military glory and its honorific trappings. Napoleon's decree of 13 July 1804 laid down that, at formal state ceremonies, the marshals should process ahead of senators and councillors of state. Lieutenants-general were similarly to have precedence over presidents of the appeal courts, archbishops, prefects, and presidents of assize courts; brigadiers-general over bishops, sub-prefects and presidents of tribunals; and subaltern officers, finally, over all other civil officials [91: 97].

A comparable analysis of the motivation and social origins, status and rewards of Napoleon's rank and file is altogether more difficult, *pace* Jean Morvan, whose major work on 'the Imperial soldier' early this century remains a classic source [100]. Unquestionably, the vast mass of common soldiers was drawn from young males of the poorer classes, above all from the peasantry. The integration of the volunteer with the regular contingents went back to the Revolutionary *amalgame* of February 1793 [90, 102], while the most important ground rules for military recruitment itself had been laid down in the Jourdan–Delbrel Law of 5 September 1798, which established conscription. Its central supervision was entrusted to special sections within the ministry of war, one of which was managed by the long-serving Hargenvilliers (1798–1814). In times of national emergency all eligible males were potentially liable to military service for an unlimited period. At other times volunteers were to be recruited for four years and faced renewal for two more, but if this proved insufficient to man all the ranks, conscription would fill the annual quotas. For the purpose, all Frenchmen upon reaching the age of twenty constituted the 'class' of that particular year, and thereafter were subject to the draft until the age of twenty-five.

Although Napoleon amended the Jourdan–Delbrel Law in several details between 1799 and 1808, he retained its basic provisions and eventually codified these and all subsequent military regulations in 1811 [24]. Under the strict terms of the 1798 law, for example, exemptions were allowed to men who had married, as well as to those who had been widowed or divorced provided that they had dependent children, on or before 12 January 1798. In practice, however, there seems to have been a fair margin of leniency towards men who married after that date, indeed towards breadwinners more generally, and their legal immunity was explicitly recognised by the *senatus-consultum* of 10 September 1808. The resort to marriage as a way of avoiding conscription thereafter became common, especially under the late Empire. Until 1812–13, furthermore, the state allowed those with adequate means to buy their way out of the draft by providing paid 'substitutes'. In spite of variations from region to region and from year to year, the going price seems to have risen from an average of 2000 francs in 1805 to 5000 in 1813 [10: *127*]. The system of 'substitutes', at first regarded as a pragmatic concession, was established as a legal right on 18 May 1802. The beneficiaries, not surprisingly, were predominantly from well-to-do bourgeois families.

Under Napoleon, the formal power of voting the annual contingent and apportioning the quotas among the departments was given initially to the legislative body, but as from 24 September 1805 it was transferred to the senate. Similarly, administrative responsibility for drawing up the lists of those eligible and enforcing the quotas lay at first with the departmental and municipal authorities, but here too there were important changes during the later Consulate and early Empire. In an attempt to remedy local negligence, vagaries and abuses, Napoleon gradually removed recruitment duties from the municipalities and brought them under more central control. Yet again he came to rely more and more on the prefects and sub-prefects, who were charged with overseeing the drawing up of lots. They were assisted in this operation by the itinerant recruiting boards (*conseils de recrutement*) established under the law of 6 August 1802 and on which military officers had a prominent role in implementing instructions from the central authorities. Provisioning of the army was planned in league with a number of specialised contractors, like Vanlerberghe as from 1805 [24].

What came to be known as the 'Grand Army', following Napoleon's phrase coined at Boulogne before the campaign of that year, might be defined as the core French units and the various foreign contingents serving under his immediate command in the field. It was appreciably larger than the armies of the old regime but actually smaller than some of those raised during the Revolution, notably under the mass levies after August 1793. Estimates of the size of the Grand Army before the decisive battles of 1805–7 vary considerably. G.E. Rothenberg cites one source giving a total of over 600,000 officers and men at the end of 1804, but also David Chandler's much lower figure of some 350,000 by 1805, and himself prefers the latter [101: *127–8*]. According to a more recent account, the draft raised an annual average of some 73,000 men between 1800 and 1810, so that from 1805 onwards the standing army was usually between 500,000 and 600,000 strong, including all foreign contingents. Even the celebrated Grand Army which marched to Russia in 1812 counted not much more than 611,000 men, and it was only during the final desperate campaigns to defend the Empire in 1813–14 that the draft began to approach a million, on paper at least [10: *23*].

By then, Napoleon was drawing deeply on reserves with little combat experience. These included the cohorts of National Guards which he had set up before his departure for Russia, the various 'Guards of Honour' consisting mostly of the sons of rich families who were drafted into the cavalry, and naval ratings summarily transferred into the field artillery. In all, though estimates still vary, it seems probable that about 2.6 million men were mustered during the Consulate and Empire [10: *126*]. Rothenberg puts that figure at less than 7 per cent of the total population of 'old France' and adds that in any case only about 1.5 million of those drafted actually enlisted [101: *134–5*]. Even after the additional levies of 1812 and 1813, the composite total in the field amounted to only a little more than two-fifths of the eligible male population, and again the proportion varied greatly from department to department [24: *200–1*].

To attain such figures, Napoleon had four sources of recruitment. There was, first, the population of 'old France', which generally provided from a third to two-fifths of the total. The non-French departments under direct annexation raised the proportion of the Imperial contingents, strictly defined, to around two-thirds. Auxiliaries from the satellite and allied states of Germany, Italy, Holland (itself annexed in 1810) and Poland accounted for most of the remaining third. Lastly, a number of foreign deserters or volunteers – Irish, Hanoverian, Swiss, Prussian, Portuguese and others – rallied to Napoleon and were usually integrated with the French units. He also had personal command of the army cavalry reserve, the artillery reserve, and of course the Imperial Guard. The Imperial headquarters itself had three divisions, the most important of which was the *Maison*, or the emperor's personal staff, the others being the general staff of the Grand Army (under Berthier) and the staff of the commissary general. To meet the deficiencies experienced in earlier campaigns, Napoleon created nine transport battalions in 1807, and a network of staging posts (*étapes*) was also introduced. As for military training, the École Polytechnique had a particularly important role in the instruction of artillery officers and engineers, and the school at Saint-Germain in that of the cavalry. The new École Spéciale Militaire founded for cadets at Fontainebleau in 1803, then transferred to Saint-Cyr in 1808, had turned out some 4000 officers by 1815 [101].

There was of course another side to this coin. Not all recruits were devoted warriors under the Eagles. The Grand Army, like all armies, had its share of anti-heroes. Georges Lefebvre's view that military defaulters posed a serious problem only after the setback in Russia soon established itself in textbooks. Of the 1.3 million men drafted between 1800 and 1812, he seemed to imply, the number of defaulters may not have exceeded the 3 per cent specifically recorded for the Côte-d'Or in the years 1806–10 [24: *200–1*]. Now, it had always been clear that the problem, which involved draft evasion as well as desertion from the ranks, increased in 1813–14. Yet if one accepts the evidence of E.A. Arnold Jr, such difficulties were endemic much earlier under Napoleon [87]. Drawing on Fouché's daily bulletins at the ministry of police, and taking as his sample period the nineteen months from December 1804 to July 1806, when Napoleon's popularity was high following Ulm and Austerlitz, Arnold found that disturbances connected with military conscription then occurred in 53 departments. The incidents were most serious and extensive in those which lay on or near the Spanish frontier. Of the various forms of military disobedience, desertion was the most troublesome, and it has long been accepted that its incidence was closely related to the agricultural cycle, especially at harvest time. Fouché himself estimated that the number of deserters in the departments most affected (the Ariège, Haute-Garonne, Basses-Pyrénées, Haute-Vienne, Ardèche, Gironde, Landes and Deux-Sèvres) was around 4000 in 1806, roughly equivalent to half their combined quota for that year [42].

Extending his argument to France as a whole, Arnold thinks that the number of deserters may have averaged some 9600 a year in 1804–6. If draft evaders are also counted, and allowances are made for monthly variations, the figure would probably have exceeded 15,000 a year. Local communities often sheltered such defaulters and on occasion offered physical resistance to the gendarmes attempting arrests. The authorities reacted in various ways, most effectively it appears by quartering troops with the families of deserters. But even such measures and the severe personal penalties facing defaulters never solved the problem. In his more recent short statement on the question, Arnold suggests that the total number of draft evaders and deserters may have been as high as half a million [10: *127*]. If this rather astonishing figure is to be believed, it would have amounted to almost a fifth of the total numbers officially mobilised during the wars of the Consulate and Empire.

(iii) Napoleonic warfare

Napoleon had inherited from the Revolution not only a momentum of territorial expansion, a reconstituted and more professional officer corps, a good supply of well-trained veterans and new rules for the recruitment of his rank and file, but also a system of tactics, battle formations and weaponry (muskets, carbines, pistols, the guns and howitzers of the field artillery), whose efficacy had already been demonstrated in the wars of conquest after 1794. Indeed, this military dynamic owed much to earlier reforms and innovations implemented during the last years of the old regime, under which Napoleon had had his own initial training. He was able to build on these and the subsequent achievements of the Republican armies, bringing to a devastating art the former teachings of men like Guibert in infantry tactics, or like Gribeauval and the Du Teil brothers in the more effective use of artillery formations and of their lighter and more manoeuvrable guns. The essential background here should be stressed, since it marks another line of continuity from the old regime to the Empire. It also confirms the conclusion of many earlier writers that Napoleon was less a thorough-going innovator than the consolidator of a known and practised military craft, which he adapted brilliantly to his own needs by his genius for improvisation.

Technologically, the French wars of 1792–1815 brought no great inventions to revolutionise the art of warfare. It is true that the Chappe visual telegraph dated from the Revolutionary wars and, by linking Paris with the French frontiers, had a major potential for military communications; but its use before 1815 had been both limited and erratic. Military transport in days before the railways was bound by the old restrictions of natural power and animal traction, which in turn gave a crucial importance to the control of strategic waterways and roads, as well as to the plentiful supply of horses. In this sense the much-vaunted flexibility and speed of manoeuvre, so often seen as the key to Napoleon's great engine of war, had more in common with the armies of the old regime – with those of Frederick the Great, for example – than with the revolution in transport wrought later by the railways. Even the efficacy of Napoleon's celebrated artillery can be exaggerated. The range of his guns remained limited, on average to half a mile, and his gun/soldier ratio (3 per 1000) was not much better than that of the old regime [10: *23*].

Of all the strategic and tactical changes brought by the French wars, the most important might be described as organisational, affecting the corps (the largest units), infantry divisions, regiments and battalions, the cavalry brigades (heavy and light), the companies of artillery and of engineers alike, along with the medical and service units. One major development was the deployment of more or less self-contained divisions to achieve greater mobility and flexibility of manoeuvre. Another was the greater use of free-moving skirmishers – fusiliers, grenadiers and light infantrymen (*voltigeurs* or *tirailleurs*) – and of the cavalry for scouting, screening and on occasion as shock troops. Improvements in artillery weapons and methods similarly enabled the French armies to establish local superiority of fire-power in battle, while the formation of mobile columns (the *ordre profond*) in place of the old serried battle-lines (*ordre mince*) gave them the advantage of what amounted to shock troops for attack. A skilful combination of the two (*ordre mixte*), as advocated by Guibert, took shape in the battalion column of 840 men, proved effective against the massed lines of enemy formations in the 1790s, and became a vital part of Napoleon's own tactics.

Napoleon used various battle-plans for attack from positions of both numerical superiority and inferiority. In the former case, he would often adopt the tactics of envelopment, including manoeuvres on the rear, to surround the enemy positions and cut off all lines of retreat. In the latter, often seen as his 'classic' tactics, an initial position of numerical inferiority could soon be turned around. He would send out advance guards of skirmishers to identify an enemy position and engage its front, while building up and concealing his own main army and nearby reserves. Then, while launching a frontal assault on the opposing forces, he would move units to attack the enemy flank, sometimes establishing local superiority there, and threaten to cut communications between the enemy front, flank and back-up depots. When enemy troops were withdrawn to strengthen the flank and secure communications, the front became more vulnerable to a massed French attack. As soon as the enemy lines showed cracks, the French reserves of heavy cavalry, artillery and even on occasion the Imperial Guard would quickly penetrate them, opening the way for the light cavalry to turn retreat into a rout.

In this way, in confronting the successive Allied Coalitions raised against him, Napoleon's aim was to attack and destroy the main armies of his enemies in short, sharp wars. It is equally clear that such strategy depended on flexible and mobile units which could be moved into one position or transferred to another quickly. This Napoleon achieved mainly by his introduction of larger mobile corps, which were in effect small armies on their own. The creation of such combat corps was certainly his major innovation in the field. These in turn required commanders of higher rank than divisional general, and here the marshals came into their own, enjoying an importance and status above all other superior officers. In fact, Napoleon's standard corps averaged from 20,000 to 30,000 men, relatively self-contained, and was usually commanded by a marshal. It was the basis of his quadrilateral formation known as the *bataillon carré*, in which several corps marched independently on campaign but within mutually supporting distance.

So, too, of all the formations serving Napoleon, the Imperial Guard had a special place in the heroic annals and mythology of the Grand Army [93, 98]. Formally created as a *corps d'élite* in July 1804, it was at first made up of chosen favourites who had accompanied him to Italy and/or Egypt, along with proven veterans of the Guard of the Directory and of the Consular Guard. With smaller units added, it consisted initially of around 8000 men. The number rose from 12,000 in 1805 to 56,000 at the time of the Russian campaign, not least by the inclusion of many foreigners. By the early months of 1814 it had swollen to over 112,000, when its various units of infantry, artillery, cavalry, service and medical corps, plus trains, reached their height [101: *145*]. Over the same period the functions of the Guard were considerably widened, so that by the end it had come to resemble a little cosmopolitan army of its own and was almost a social microcosm of the Imperial military hierarchy, with its own preferential system of rewards and privileges, rank for rank. The extraordinary sense of honour and mystique surrounding it was intensified by the dramatic events of the Hundred Days and the second abdication, and it lived on in the Napoleonic legend as an evocative symbol of past grandeur. Yet as an actual combat force the Guard was only sparingly used, and then always as a last reserve, to terrify the enemy and add lustre to the hour of victory. Conversely, its disintegration at Waterloo, when it took the field in greatly reduced number, had the opposite effect on the morale of the French troops.

It is however fair to add that Napoleon's tactical genius was also, in an ironic way, its own source of weakness in his armies, taken as a whole. The key to his success in so many decisive encounters lay in his imaginative improvisation on the field of battle. This was where the combination of those qualities of intellect and temperament he considered 'a gift from heaven' was put to the test. As he later reminisced to General Gourgaud in exile, 'my great talent, the one that distinguishes me the most, is to see the entire picture distinctly'. Once he had conceived the general plan, he would adjust it to the needs of particular campaigns or battles. But he was also loath to share such a prerogative with others, even with some of his marshals. When removed from his immediate presence and forced to conduct their own campaigns, too many of his generals, most notably in Spain and Portugal, proved deficient in skill and judgement. This was due not least to his own reluctance to share commanding authority. As one of his marshals, Berthier, informed another, Ney, in 1807: 'the Emperor needs neither advice nor plans of campaign. Nobody knows his thoughts and our duty is to obey.'

At the same time, Napoleon's own military successes did not lack a certain makeshift quality. Some of the older campaign histories imply that he had devised detailed battle-plans for all situations, and that his great victories were achieved by following them closely. A more recent reassessment by Owen Connelly, whose general tenor is nicely subsumed in its title, *Blundering to Glory*, shows on the contrary just how far and how often Napoleon departed from preconceived plans in particular encounters. His genius, and the key to his superiority over so many enemy commanders, lay precisely in this capacity for bold tactical improvisation on campaign and specifically in the heat of battle. In other words, he triumphed more by immediate pragmatic flair, by his unique ability to inspire his men, to redeem a weakened position, and to exploit the critical errors of his opponents, than by a rigid adherence to theoretical blueprints. Luck also had a part to play here; so on a number of occasions did the services of able subordinates like Davout (for instance at Austerlitz, Auerstädt and Eckmühl) and Masséna (at different times in Italy, Switzerland, Poland and Austria, before his eventual disgrace in Portugal) [96].

It seems, too, that Napoleon's tactical advantage over his enemies lessened as the period advanced. As his seasoned troops were thinned out by steady attrition, at first during the victorious campaigns of 1805–7, and then with much less successful results in the Peninsula, so he was forced to rely more and more on inexperienced recruits and on foreign auxiliaries. British commanders were quick to learn from French methods, and in time were to turn them against Napoleon's armies themselves. His tactical innovations became notably less effective as from 1808, and his subsequent victories were often narrower and more costly in men than in the earlier campaigns. At Aspern-Essling (21–22 May 1809), for instance, he relied more on crude massed charges than on tactical finesse, and if he avenged that French defeat at Wagram soon afterwards (5–6 July), it was at the cost of some 30,000 men. Similar methods at Borodino (7 September 1812) brought casualties of the same order, truly a Pyrrhic victory, and at Waterloo (18 June 1815) his storming tactics against Wellington cost 25,000 men, more than a third of his complement. Such sacrifices add a jarring note to his remarks to Joseph on 26 June 1806 that 'one always has enough troops when one knows how to use them' and, to the same correspondent on the following 18 September, that 'in war nothing is achieved except by calculation. Everything that is not soundly planned in its details yields no result' [5].

In the planning and prosecution of war it is conventional to distinguish between campaign strategy and battle tactics in the shorter term, of the kind just discussed, and 'grand strategy' in the sense of a wider overall design [9]. If there was a consistent theme in Napoleon's 'grand strategy', it surely lay in his unrelenting hostility to Britain, his most elusive and implacable enemy during this period. In meeting her challenge, whether naval, military or economic, he had eventually to accept that he could not attack her directly on the seas. In the early years, it is true, he kept alive hopes of a colonial empire in the Levant, born no doubt of his experience in Egypt. As late as 1803–5 he was still considering the possibility of a direct invasion of England from his camp in Boulogne. Whether or not this was a concerted project or rather a front to disguise his plans for the land campaigns of 1805, it certainly foundered after the French defeat at Trafalgar that year (21 October). Thereafter, his 'grand strategy' was necessarily forced back within the perimeters of the continental mainland. His Continental Blockade of 1806–13, whose economic significance is discussed in a later chapter, was one response to his land-locked power. The mechanics of its enforcement, for military and economic reasons alike, drew him into the major confrontations in the Peninsula as from 1807, into the Dutch and north German annexations of 1810–11, and eventually of course into the fatal Russian campaign of 1812.

Napoleon's foreign policy had less to do with diplomatic finesse, unless one extends the term to include his ability to browbeat conquered states and enforce one-sided punitive treaties on them, than with the creation of military vassals beyond the Imperial frontiers. Eighteenth-century notions of a 'balance of power' among European states were swept away and replaced by a more grandiose vision of French continental hegemony. Even so, it was only after his victories of 1805–7 that Napoleon was able to integrate the subject states in Italy, Germany, Holland and Poland more effectively into his military and fiscal system. The 'Grand Empire' was to be, in significant part, the servile provider of the Grand Army. Apart from the auxiliary military levies required of them, the subject states were also exposed to the French expedient of 'living off the land', which Napoleon had inherited from the Revolutionary armies and then systematised in his provisioning policy there. As from 1805, furthermore, we see a major development in his use of war as a 'good thing' – 'une bonne affaire' – at the expense of conquered states. Austria, for example, seems to have paid at least 75 of the 118 million francs demanded that year, and 164 of the 250 million imposed on her in 1809. Estimates of similar Prussian payments between 1806 and 1812 vary from 470 to 514 million, the indemnity following Jena alone accounting for 311 million, as noted earlier. Portugal, by contrast, apparently paid only 6 of the 100 million demanded in 1807, an indication of the tenuous hold Napoleon had over his Iberian subjects in the early phase of the Peninsular War [12: *647*].

It is a textbook truism that the main mistakes of Napoleon's 'grand strategy' were the Spanish and Russian ventures. The first, so much nearer home, might have been more successful if he had been able to concentrate more troops and give more of his own time to Spain, although it must be said that the terrain, climate and food resources there were not ideal for his tactics. This he was reluctant to do, and certainly he also underestimated the ferocity of the Spanish insurgents as well as the technical skills of the British commanders, Wellington foremost among them, until it was too late. The performance of the French armies in the Peninsula was erratic, at best, and King Joseph's own military pretensions did not help matters. The capitulation of Baylen (21 July 1808) in southern Spain and the battle of Vimiero to the north of Lisbon shortly afterwards (21 August), though not in themselves decisive encounters, were important blows in dispelling the myth of French invincibility. They were a spur to other states to renew hostilities, as Austria did in 1809, albeit unsuccessfully. By the end, the Peninsular War had cost France perhaps 300,000 men and 3000 million francs in gold [10: *387*].

Yet defeat in the Peninsula would not itself have been enough to bring Napoleon down. A successful Russian campaign might even have secured a far-flung eastern frontier, set up a closer alliance with Turkey, and allowed him to concentrate on a major new commitment across the Pyrenees. The mistakes of 1812 were three-fold. First, in spite of careful preparations, Napoleon had not paid enough detailed attention to the problem of securing his commissariat lines for a campaign so far removed from his base. Secondly, he mistook the Russian retreat and 'scorched-earth' policy for a sign of weakness in his enemy, or at least for delaying tactics. Lastly, he seems to have supposed after the costly victory at Borodino that a decisive battle for Moscow would deliver the tsar into his hands, when the sheer size of Russia in fact allowed Alexander and his commanders several inaccessible havens of retreat.

The result was that Napoleon stayed in Moscow too long, did not get the decisive showdown he sought, and exposed his exhausted army in its retreat to the counter-attacks of troops more familiar with the terrain and which could

71

exploit the impasse created by the Russian winter. Though estimates vary, the total losses suffered by the French and their allies in deaths, prisoners and deserters during this campaign alone were around 380,000 [32: *304*]. The loss of field guns and of horses was the heaviest on record in a single campaign. One of the lessons of 1812 was that France, even with her continental vassals, had not sufficient resources to sustain major wars on two fronts, themselves so far apart. The loyalty of those vassals themselves was not boundless, as the defection of several German states to the Allied Coalition in 1813–14 was to show. Without such military props the 'Grand Empire', so assiduously built up over seven or eight years, finally fell apart in rather less than one.

5 The Formation and Endowment of an Imperial Élite

(i) Nobles and *notables**

The most original and important research in Napoleonic studies during the past thirty years has been concerned with social structures. How well did the Empire assimilate the old nobility? How successfully did it advance the social status and professional expectations of other sorts of *notables*? What, within the Napoleonic social élites, was the relative importance of civilian and military *notables*? How did Napoleon's system of rewards work? Where did he find the means to launch that system at all? Did he have what might be called a 'social policy', and if so, how lasting did it prove to be?

To answer such questions, we must start with the land settlement of the Revolution. Both in the Concordat (concerning Church lands) and in the Civil Code (concerning émigré property) the principle was clearly enunciated that those who had bought the various issues of confiscated land would not be dispossessed of them, and that their former owners would not be entitled to compensation. In fact, the provisions of the Civil Code on landownership under this heading were partly recapitulatory statements, since the legal position of émigré property had been defined earlier

---

* A diagrammatic representation of the Imperial social hierarchy is given in Appendix I; Appendix II lists the chief appointments and honours bestowed by Napoleon, including all the marshals; and Appendix III names the ten 'grand dignitaries' of the Empire.

in the Consulate. An *arrêté* of 20 October 1800 had lifted the sequestration on the lands of émigrés whose names had been eliminated from the proscribed list. This was confirmed by a *senatus-consultum* of 26 April 1802, with the exception of woodlands and forests already declared inalienable by the law of 25 December 1795, for reasons of national defence, and of buildings already put to public use. On the other hand, the *arrêté* of 18 July 1800 had declared as irrevocable all sales of *biens nationaux* hitherto effected at the expense of émigrés, even if they were or were about to be excluded from the prohibited list [108].

Since land remained the basis of social pre-eminence as well as of economic weight, realignments within the French property market during the 1790s had had important social consequences. As a rule, the main beneficiaries among the *'acquéreurs des biens nationaux'* had been the bourgeoisie and the better-off peasantry. As they already possessed land or other capital assets producing disposable income, they had the means to advance their holdings. As a result of these changes, the Church had ceased to be a corporate proprietor, while the abolition of the monarchy, tax farms, guilds and trading monopolies had brought additional amounts of property under national ownership.

It is less clear how much émigré property had similarly been sold off. Robert Forster estimates that the old nobility, or *'ci-devants'* as they were often dubbed, had owned about a quarter of all French land before the Revolution, plus the title to many lucrative seigneurial dues. The abolition of these dues and the émigré land confiscations may have deprived them, on average, of between a fifth and a quarter of their former wealth and income. If anything, such losses had been more severe among nobles living in Paris than among their provincial colleagues [109]. On the other hand, most of the old nobility had not emigrated or suffered outright confiscations. The émigrés themselves appear to have recovered perhaps as much as a quarter of their confiscated property through various legal ruses before Brumaire, or else did so under the Napoleonic amnesties. In all, if the old nobility had indeed been reduced in wealth, income and influence as a result of the Revolutionary laws, they were still the largest individual landowners in most regions of France during the Empire, not least in Paris [144]. Whether active or not in the public life of the Napoleonic state, the '*ci-devants*' still *mattered* in the society of that time.

Yet it is also clear that the great majority of the old second estate, variously estimated at between 200,000 and 300,000 on the eve of the Revolution, did not seek and did not in fact play a prominent role in public life under Napoleon. The émigrés in particular had personal reasons for their circumspection towards him. Their priorities were more private and practical: to return to their families, to salvage what they could of their inheritance, and to rebuild their shattered estates. The case of the marquis de Lafayette well illustrates their motives. During the Consulate he was offered first the American embassy and then a seat in the senate, membership of the Legion of Honour, or at least important office in his department, but he declined them all. If we lack detailed studies of the behaviour of returned émigrés under Napoleon, perhaps this is precisely because they then eschewed public prominence. There is little evidence to suggest that they rallied *en masse* to his service.

Can the same be said of the old nobility as a whole? We have already noted their importance in the officer corps of the army. Other, perhaps more telling, examples of nobles who joined Napoleon's service might also be cited: Philippe comte de Ségur, Albert duc de Luynes, Louis comte de Narbonne, the duc de Broglie (who died in 1804), Talleyrand-Périgord and Mathieu-Louis Molé, the former *parlementaire*. One could similarly add the names of families which in 1789 had been only recently ennobled (*anoblis*): Marmont, Rémusat, Berthier and Roederer, for instance. Appointments to the post of chamberlain within the Imperial household sometimes gave preference to old noble families like d'Aubusson de la Feuillade, Croy, Mercy-Argentau, Choiseul-Praslin, Turenne and d'Haussonville, while the ménage of the empress also had names like Rohan, La Rochefoucauld, Montmorency, Rochechouart-Mortemart and Bouillé. In part, this was a story of aristocratic realism, of professional survival, often involving personal adjustments to a new public role.

75

It seems, too, that many more of the old nobility were willing to come forward after the inauguration of the Imperial titles in March 1808, and especially after Napoleon's marriage alliance with Austria in 1810. In his social analyses of Napoleon's prefects and diplomats, E.A. Whitcomb found that those of old noble origin were more numerous during the later Empire than earlier [53, 54]. In the prefectoral corps, for instance, the high-point was reached in 1814, when 53 incumbents (43 per cent of the total) were former nobles, and when they also occupied a disproportionate number of the more important posts. On the other hand, Whitcomb also found that the quickest *rate* of noble appointments to prefectures had actually come during the earlier years, when their proportion rose from 23 per cent in 1800 to 37 per cent in 1807. Their later influx must then have been in newly formed Imperial departments rather than at the expense of incumbent bourgeois, whose absolute number remained largely stable over the whole period, though falling proportionally from 77 per cent (77 prefects) in 1800 to 57 per cent (71 prefects) in 1814 [53: *1094*]. Finally, when the lists of the 'most distinguished' citizens (*les personnes les plus marquantes*) were drawn up in each department during the later years, roughly a fifth of those named were nobles of the old regime [106]. Some accepted new titles of the Imperial nobility.

Such noble 'ralliés', if the term does not overstate their true motives, were nevertheless the exception rather than the rule. They made up only a small fraction of the former second estate in France. Most of their order, perhaps as many as 80 or even 90 per cent, evidently preferred not to be publicly identified with Napoleon's regime. While much has been made of his policy of 'careers open to talents' and of his 'politics of amalgamation', it appears that the old nobility in large part remained a missing or reluctant ingredient of that process. In another essay I have called them 'the low-profile *notables*' or '*non-dramatis personae*' of the Empire, an element of the group sometimes referred to as 'the émigrés of the interior'. Their consent was to be inferred only from their silence [108].

For the same reason one may well question Tulard's claim

that the Imperial nobility 'prepared the fusion of the old nobility and a bourgeois élite' [113: *658*]. This is perhaps too official and top-heavy a view of 'notability' under Napoleon, and in any case it would seem applicable mainly to the later Empire. Any suggestion that the 'fusion' implied 'marriage', as it were in community of property, should be discounted. The membership of the departmental electoral colleges had a much smaller representation of former nobles than the 20 per cent or so recorded among '*les plus marquantes*', 'the most notable of the *notables*', of 1812–14. Tulard himself estimates that nobles accounted for less than 3 per cent of the first lists of 'notabilities' drawn up under the consular law of 4 March 1801 [115: *26*]. In their joint work on the *notables* of five French departments at the height of the Empire, Louis Bergeron, Guy Chaussinand-Nogaret and Robert Forster found that the old nobility, here admittedly defined in the rather restricted sense of 'the old landed aristocracy', were numerically insignificant in the departmental and arrondissement electoral colleges of 1810 [104].

Napoleon's later social promotions, or what has sometimes been called his 'rehierarchisation' of French society, were also part of an elaborate dynastic policy. As such, it necessarily involved the subject states, and here again the years 1805–7 were crucial. Without the military victories and constitutional innovations of that time, there could have been no 'Grand Empire'. Without their spoils, the new Imperial titles would have lacked the material substance of land-gifts and other rewards. It was primarily in the conquered territories of Italy, Germany and Poland that Napoleon found the lands and rents with which to endow his beneficiaries (*donataires*) with land-gifts (*dotations*) [110]. Given the scale of these endowments, it is tempting to conclude that Napoleon had decided to break with the Revolutionary principle of legal equality at least from the time of his Legion of Honour and senatoriates of 1802–3, to which appointments were made for life. The proclamation of the Empire was accompanied by the creation of its six 'grand dignitaries' and of the ten 'grand civil officers' of the Imperial household. Indeed, the seeds of this grandiose policy can be found still earlier in Napoleon's distribution of 'arms of honour' for prominent services at Brumaire or in the second Italian campaign. Yet the case for a more gradual and pragmatic application of his dynastic placements and social promotions rests on the fact that he had inherited a Revolutionary land settlement which could *not* be undone. In 1802–4 he quite simply did not have a stock of disposable lands within 'old France' with which to fuel his spoils system on anything like the later scale.

As for that, by the time of the first abdication in April 1814, the Legion of Honour had over 32,000 members, which of course had greatly diluted both its social exclusiveness and its material rewards. It had become in large part a decorative institution for faithful soldiers, who made up as much as 95 per cent of its complement. This was certainly the principal route by which military officers and men could gain social honours. By contrast, surprisingly few officers of high rank (generals or colonels) and still fewer of lower rank (sub-lieutenants, lieutenants or captains) were named in the lists of the 100,000 *notables* of the Empire, as analysed in the computerised study of Bergeron and Chaussinand-Nogaret [105]. Greater social pre-eminence undoubtedly attached to the Imperial titles themselves, and here the top brass of the army *was* well represented. These were multiplied in an elaborate hierarchy after the two decrees of 1 March 1808, although their origins again lay earlier.

Apart from the princes appointed in 1804, there were the twenty-two 'ducal grand-fiefs' (*duchés grands-fiefs de l'Empire*) created by a series of decrees on 30 March 1806. Twelve were carved out of the Venetian lands ceded by Austria after the defeats of 1805 and then 'reunited' with the new Kingdom of Italy. They were to be convertible into hereditary estates under French law (*majorats de droit français*) by male primogeniture, could not be sold or otherwise alienated except with Napoleon's express permission, and were made over to a select group of his marshals and other military chiefs or ministers. Six more were created in the new kingdom of Naples from the dispossessed assets of the Spanish Bourbons, and the rest from lands variously centred on Massa-Carrara, Parma and Piacenza. These were similarly convertible into *majorats* for the benefit of Imperial dignitaries, including members of Napoleon's family. At the same time a sum of 1.2 million francs a year payable from the *Monte Napoleone*, a bank founded in 1805 to consolidate and liquidate the Italian public debt, was earmarked for distribution among favoured *donataires*. Another decree of the same date granted the principality of Guastalla to Pauline, Napoleon's sister, and it too became a *majorat* [110].

The March decrees of 1808 created the titles of count, baron and chevalier of the Empire and laid down the criteria for elevations into the new nobility. Two routes were envisaged: the titles would be granted either by virtue of civil office exercised or else at the sovereign's pleasure for military or civil services to the state. The eldest sons of the 'grand dignitaries' of the Empire were to be dukes of the Empire by right. Ministers, senators, councillors of state for life, presidents of the legislative body and archbishops were to be counts of the Empire by right. In the same way, presidents of departmental electoral colleges, mayors of large cities, bishops and some other civil officials were to be barons, and members of the Legion of Honour chevaliers, of the Empire by the first route. By means of the second, Napoleon reserved the right to grant whatever titles he judged appropriate to generals, prefects, civil and military officers, and to any others who 'have distinguished themselves by services to the State'. A qualifying income was also required of all recipients of such titles: 200,000 francs a year for dukes, 30,000 for counts, 15,000 for barons, 3000 for chevaliers. In order to establish a *majorat* by right of male primogeniture, the title-holder had to give evidence of an additional hereditary income, either in landed property or in state securities or Bank shares. The qualifying sums were set here at 20,000 francs for dukes, 10,000 for counts, and 5000 for barons, but chevaliers were excluded from these particular provisions [107].

What made the difference between the carefully restricted endowments of 1802–6 and the much more numerous titles and land-gifts after 1808 was precisely the military and political subjugation of Italy, Germany and Poland, where the lands and revenues of the former feudal princes were turned over to Napoleon's use. Unlike those of the old regime, the Imperial titles were intended, initially at least, to be personal rewards for military or civilian service to the state. If the qualifying income at each rung of the noble hierarchy restricted the total number of ennoblements, in many cases, most notably in the army, the Imperial *dotations* were actually intended to provide the means for such qualification. Jean Tulard, limiting himself to proven archival records of titles granted by Napoleon's letters patent or express decree between 1808 and 1815, lists a total of at least 3364 Imperial nobles, excluding members of the Bonaparte family and those related to it by marriage. The actual figure was probably nearer 3600, since allowance must be made for archival omissions. The distribution of titles in Tulard's alphabetical list sub-divides as follows: 34 princes and dukes, 459 counts, 1552 barons, and 1319 chevaliers of the Empire [115]. The latter need to be distinguished from the much more numerous chevaliers of the Legion of Honour, whose automatic elevation into the Imperial nobility itself ceased in 1810, when it was decreed that their titles might be so recognised only at the third transmission [107].

The result, by 1814, was that hereditary titles had been confined to some 200 heads of family, while the Imperial nobility as a whole numbered only about one-seventh of its royal counterpart of 1789 [16: *69*]. According to Tulard, some 22.5 per cent of the Imperial nobles were of the old nobility, 58 per cent of bourgeois origin, while 19.5 per cent (invariably borne aloft by the great motor of the army) came from the popular classes. If the same group is analysed by professional occupation, the preponderance of military men is again apparent at once. Some 59 per cent were in that category, all the marshals and most of the lieutenants-general and brigadiers-general receiving the title of count or baron, while 387 colonels became barons and 146 company-grade officers chevaliers of the Empire. By comparison, 22 per cent of the Imperial titles went to higher civil servants (councillors of state, prefects, bishops, inspectors, magistrates); 17 per cent to *notables* of other sorts (senators, members of the departmental electoral colleges, and mayors); 1.5 per cent to men grouped under the heading of 'talents' (doctors, academics, members of the Institute, archivists, sculptors, composers and the like); and only 0.5 per cent to those in trade and industry [115].

All this, moreover, was just the cream of the social hierarchy; many more lesser *notables* made up the homogeneous milk lower down. By January 1810 there were upwards of 4000 *donataires* who in theory enjoyed land-gifts worth more than 18 million francs a year in rents. By April 1814 the figures had risen to nearly 6000 and 30 million francs respectively. In provincial France, beyond the titles and rewards of the civil and military establishments, the social origins of the *notables* were more diverse. In their cited study of five representative departments in 1810, Bergeron, Chaussinand-Nogaret and Forster gathered a sample of more than 3700 members of the departmental and arrondissement electoral colleges. Of the 2518 whose occupations could be identified, much the largest groups were in the liberal professions or trade, in the administrative or judicial services, and in agriculture (*propriétaires agriculteurs*). The common denominator was ownership of property, and there appears to have been a striking stability of careers within the main professional groups [104].

It is difficult to give an exact figure for the total number of *notables* in the French Empire at its height. If one includes all whose names appeared on the lists of the departmental electoral colleges and on those of the *'plus imposés'*, then an estimate of 75,000 or more seems reasonable. Bergeron and Chaussinand-Nogaret, as we have seen, give a round figure of 100,000 in their study of the *'masses de granit'*, as Napoleon himself once called them; but in reaching it they had to trawl deeply into the shoals of the arrondissement as well as the departmental electoral colleges [105]. That figure includes men of widely differing wealth, the great majority of them far removed from the immediate *éclat* of the Imperial entourage. As the 'granite' metaphor suggests, they were supposed to be the plinths and columns of a glorious monument, but a great many in fact could hardly aspire to such imposing stature. Nevertheless, whether large or small fry, these were the *notables* who collectively formed the social élite of the Napoleonic Empire.

(ii) The treatment of the annexed lands and subject states

Since the annexed territories were officially assimilated to French law, while the subject states became vital functions of Napoleon's dynastic placements abroad and social promotions within the Empire itself, we need to look more closely at his treatment of both. The old view that he was a systematic rationaliser and in that sense a social reformer dies hard. Following its line, the imperial 'recess' of the German Diet in February 1803 and the creation of the Confederation of the Rhine in July 1806 were all necessary stages in the process of their 'defeudalisation'. Affecting political, administrative, ecclesiastical, judicial, military, social and economic institutions alike, this process was the nearest thing at the time to 'modernisation'. Without it, German economic union and then political unification would not have been possible during the next fifty or sixty years. The Napoleonic experience is thus seen as the necessary prelude to a modern German state. *Mutatis mutandis*, the same argument has also been made for Napoleon's impact on Italy.

More recent studies of Napoleonic Germany and Italy, however, have questioned and qualified such conclusions on several important points. There are, first, the elementary facts of chronology. Neither country was exposed all at once, or for the same length of time, to effective French rule. The whole process of their subjugation and reorganisation came in stages, themselves largely determined by prior military conquest and the terms of subsequent treaties. Similarly, the subject states of Germany and Italy were not brought under French rule in a single uniform way. Distinctions also need to be made between the different constitutional forms of subjugation.

Some territories, as we have seen, were *directly* annexed to France relatively early under Napoleon. In Germany, these were the lands west of the Rhine, administered by prefects directly responsible to Paris, which in due course were also to be included in the 25th and 26th military divisions, where recruitment applied as for any other part of the French

Empire. In theory, they were exposed to the full application of the new codes, notably the *Code Napoléon*. In principle, too, their merchants and manufacturers had free access to the large Imperial home market, since the French customs frontier had been officially extended to the Rhine in July 1798. The corresponding areas of Italy were Piedmont and the Ligurian coast, Savoy and Nice having been fully incorporated into France during the Revolution. Together, the Piedmontese and Ligurian departments formed the 27th and a large part of the 28th military divisions of the Empire. Other German and Italian states, secondly, were ruled by Frenchmen appointed by Napoleon, and though wholly dependent on his continuing favours, were nominally distinct from the French Empire itself. The kingdoms of Italy, of Naples, of Westphalia, and the grand duchy of Berg were the most prominent here. A third category consisted of allied states governed by their own native sovereigns and élites, of which the most important were the kingdoms of Bavaria, of Württemberg, of Saxony, and the grand duchy of Baden.

In the technical language of the time, the distinctions which have just been made are between the '*pays réunis*', the '*pays conquis*' and the '*pays alliés*' of Germany and Italy. Attempts to apply the Napoleonic codes to most of those regions should, hypothetically, have reformed their existing institutions under French law. The constitutions of the subject states nominally upheld that principle as well, even to the point of assuming the deed from the advertised intent. But we may well ask whether those official aims were in fact achieved, whether Napoleon succeeded in rationalising and 'modernising' the legal, social and economic systems of the subject lands. Alternatively, we need to know how far he was inhibited by his military and dynastic needs from carrying such policies through to their logical conclusion there, how far time itself was the enemy of fundamental reform, and how far in the event he made a pragmatic compromise with the old feudal structures and privileged élites in order to extract his Imperial spoils.

In answering these questions we must again start with Napoleon's inheritance in France itself. The formal legal position is clear enough and can be stated at once. Before Brumaire, 'feudalism' had been outlawed in France in all its forms. Starting with the famous night of 4 August 1789, and ending with the decree of the National Convention of 17 July 1793, the abolition of 'feudal' dues and of the redemption payments allowed by the Constituent and Legislative Assemblies had been officially completed. The application of the same policy to Belgium, the German left bank of the Rhine and Piedmont had itself been a major factor in the widening of the Revolutionary wars. To the confiscation and sale of Church property one should thus add the formal extinction, under French law, of all former 'feudal' dues. The Concordat and the Civil Code enshrined those reforms as *faits accomplis*.

We are at 1804. Three to four years later, when the *Code Napoléon* was promulgated, or in March 1808, when the Imperial nobility was formally inaugurated on a grand scale, a wider dimension of Napoleon's power and ambition had become manifest. He now had a new alignment of German, Italian and Polish satellites to contribute to his military needs. He also had, from those same conquered lands, what the very finality of the Revolutionary land settlement in France denied him: a disposable stock of lands, or in effect *rents*, with which to endow his Imperial nobility and reward his host of lesser military faithful. These lands-as-rents in the subject states soon became the indispensable lubricant of his dynastic placements abroad and social promotions at home.

Now, from their various regional angles, several scholars have questioned whether the effects of Napoleon's dynastic placements, fiscal levies and land-gifts were consistent with the aim of exporting his codes. French policy in this respect might be assessed in a number of ways. The first and most important is to determine how far the official abolition of feudal practices (that is, payment of seigneurial dues in cash or kind, and a whole variety of personal obligations) had been carried through in the annexed lands and subject states by the end of the Empire. Secondly, one might estimate the extent to which the dispossession of feudal princes, and the transfer of their dues to Imperial beneficiaries, actually freed their vassals from traditional obligations in those regions. Thirdly, one might measure the impact of the Napoleonic codes on old professional groups and practices there, for instance on exclusive trade guilds and other privileged corporations. Finally, one might identify the social groups which benefited most from the sale of confiscated property outside France.

If these four criteria are applied, it is clear that the French impact was greatest in those parts of Germany and Italy which lay closest to France and were also exposed longest to her reformed laws and professional practices. By 1814, the departments of the German left bank of the Rhine and of Piedmont-Liguria had all experienced important institutional changes through their formal assimilation to French rule. Their treatment as lands directly ruled from Paris might be compared with that of Belgium, which had been annexed to France earlier still in 1795 [123]. They could be seen as territorial extensions of 'old France' and, in that sense, as vital parts of her organic life under Napoleon. Apart from the sale of nationalised Church property, they were officially incorporated into the military divisions and prefectoral system of the Consulate and Empire. They also formed an integral part of all the other institutions of the Napoleonic state: treasury inspectorates, chambers of commerce, grain markets, bridges and highways, mining divisions, trade tribunals, industrial arbitration councils, the whole apparatus of civil and criminal courts, the diocesan structure of the concordatory Church, the Imperial University, and so forth [11].

This is not the place to enter into the long debate on the kicks and kindnesses of French rule in all the annexed lands. The balance between 'pessimists' who stress the evidence of outright exploitation and 'optimists' who point instead to the material advantages experienced under Napoleon suggests very mixed results [132]. But whichever way the scale is tipped, two themes are constant: the *continuity* within the evolving social and professional élites of the annexed territories, and the often *conservative* results of French policy there. Two regional illustrations must suffice here. The first is the area of the Rhenish left bank which became the Roer

85

department under French rule and, after 1815, the north-western part of the Prussian Rhine Provinces. In his study of the 'businessmen' of Cologne, Crefeld and Aachen over the whole period from 1789 to 1834, Jeffry Diefendorf speaks of their 'early liberalism' and argues that concrete experience of French rule 'provided an important part of the German bourgeoisie with a lasting and fateful political education' [124: *17*]. On the other hand, he also shows how they defended many of their old privileges by adapting to the various forms of French and then Prussian rule, surviving and even prospering as essentially pragmatic patriots, and how their political masters in both the parent states made allowances for their local customs and traditional interests. Such continuity reflects in the careers of some who, having served the French, like Bernard Boisserée, J.P. Heimann, G.H. Koch and P.H. Merkens, all luminaries of the chamber of commerce in Cologne, went on to work with the Prussians. Yet it is as staunch defenders of *local* interests (of Cologne's commercial staple, for instance, finally abolished only in 1831), that the businessmen of Diefendorf's study stand out most prominently.

The second example is Rosalba Davico's account of the *notables* of Piedmont between 1750 and 1816, which also stresses the social continuities, conservative as well as reformist, and establishes that much had been achieved in the way of 'defeudalisation' there well before the application of French law. Freehold property (*terres allodiales*) had become the preponderant sort at least a century before Napoleon, which could certainly not be said of Italy as a whole. It had also become the almost exclusive source of state taxes. One effect of French rule was thus to give 'legal consecration' to the material improvement of many local 'mini-élites' which had evolved within proprietary relationships since the mid-eighteenth century. With the sale of the *biens nationaux*, however, the wealthier hegemonic élites unquestionably monopolised the market. If its tax exemptions are taken into account, Church property had made up about a fifth of the total landed revenue of Piedmont in the early eighteenth century. By the same reckoning, the allodial lands of the nobility had then represented another 10 per cent of that total, excluding seigneurial dues, and most of it was not to be confiscated and sold under the French [122].

Over the whole period from 1798 to 1810 the sales of *biens nationaux* in the 27th military division (which included most of Piedmont) exceeded 66 million francs, equivalent to roughly twice the average annual value of Piedmontese exports during those same years. They were dominated by a mixed group of old landowners, merchants, bankers and higher office-holders. As Davico puts it, 'the bloc of the nobility broke up only to reconstitute itself into a new élite' [122: *260*]. By comparison, the peasantry as a whole gained little. Altogether, Piedmont well illustrates what Stuart Woolf has called 'the social constraints of political change' and 'the years of Napoleonic social conservatism' in Italy. Among the Piedmontese noble families which came out well from the sale of the *biens nationaux* were the likes of Cavour, Lamarmora, Balbo and D'Azeglio, all prominent later in the Risorgimento [141].

In the Italian and German lands brought under direct French rule later, there was of course less time for the codes to be applied in the same way. If one takes the most obvious examples of Tuscany, the Papal States and Rome itself in Italy, or of the Hanse towns and the grand duchy of Oldenburg in Germany, all annexed at different times between 1808 and January 1811, they would have had only a few years in which to naturalise French law before Napoleon's first abdication. Their legal and social assimilation to French practices could not be widely extended during the short time available. Within such varying time-scales and constitutional alignments of Imperial rule, it is no wonder that the process of rationalisation and codification *à la française* was erratic and largely unfulfilled by April 1814.

If we turn now to the subject states, the Republic (1801–5) and then Kingdom of Italy (1805–14) was politically and economically the most important south of the Alps, and also had the longest exposure to French dominance. Its antecedent, the Cisalpine Republic (1797–1801), had set an early standard of subservience to and emulation of French constitutional models [130]. Eugène de Beauharnais inherited from Melzi d'Eril, vice-president of the Italian Republic, a political regime manned by moderates, but with its social roots firmly planted in conservative proprietary relationships. While sales of the *biens nationaux* were resumed, they tended to reinforce the hold of established landowners and of a plutocratic bourgeois élite. Lacking assistance from the state, smallholders were again eclipsed and also bore a disproportionate part of the land tax. On occasion the earlier reforms had actually been reversed, when for instance the allodial (as distinct from feudal) lands of nobles confiscated during the Revolutionary period were restored to their former owners in 1803 [141: 202–3]. The later application of the Napoleonic codes in the Kingdom of Italy favoured the same 'amalgamation' of old and new propertied élites, who collaborated in the spoils of office and also dominated the electoral colleges. Nobles may have lost the legal title to their seigneurial dues and other corporate privileges, but their rights as individual proprietors remained sacrosanct. They were still the foremost social magnates, and their economic hold over their tenants persisted.

Pasquale Villani's work on the Italian south similarly reveals a striking capacity among the old feudal lords to adapt to French rule and survive, specifically in the sale of state lands in the kingdom of Naples, in which the social conservatism of urban élites is also evident. The sales, which included monastic confiscations and then émigré property, began only in 1806 after the appointment of Joseph Bonaparte as king of Naples, at the time when seigneurial dues were officially abolished and the common lands divided. Yet out of a total population of some 5 million, only 2704 buyers are recorded as having participated in the sales, and 7 per cent of them engrossed 65 per cent of this market. Most of the large estates (*latifundia*) survived intact and some were actually consolidated, since the principal buyers included a number of noble grandees beside high state officials and even a few French generals like Jourdan, Camprendon and Salligny. As for the smaller buyers, a majority were of the middle and lower bourgeoisie, Neapolitan merchants most commonly, and purchases by the peasantry were comparatively insignificant. The old

88

agrarian structures were not fundamentally changed and proved strong enough to accommodate the newer element of bourgeois gentrification [139]. If allowances are made for regional variations, Villani's broader survey of the *Mezzogiorno* from the 1730s to 1860 reaches the same conclusion over all [138]. True, his textbook on Napoleonic Italy as a whole points to even greater regional and local variations in the land sales; yet if a class of bourgeois parvenus can be seen emerging alongside the old landed nobility and the established urban patriciate, especially in the larger northern towns, that process was unquestionably much less extensive or profound than it had been in France [140].

The theme of social conservatism recurs no less in Elisabeth Fehrenbach's important works on the application of the *Code Napoléon* in the various states of the Rhenish Confederation as from the summer of 1807. The Code conflicted with the local customs and vested interests of pre-revolutionary élites, and its unsettling effects appear to have been neither uniform nor generally progressive. Some states, such as the grand duchy of Frankfurt and the duchies of Nassau and Hesse, while paying lip-service to its promulgation, so reduced or qualified its clauses in practice that its official aims were altogether distorted. The kingdoms of Bavaria and of Württemberg, notionally independent and sovereign states, were in an even better position to resist its adoption in the first place. Admittedly, the debate accompanying Napoleon's attempt to impose his Code across the Rhine did generate ideas of freer and more 'bourgeois' economic enterprise which were to be of later importance in Germany. For all their shortcomings, these early lessons in legal simplification inspired the vision of a uniform code in place of the old and fragmentary feudal procedures. As such, they were to influence subsequent generations of German liberals and nationalists during the period leading up to the 1848 revolutions, most notably in Baden and in the heartland of Berg. They underlined a sharper distinction between the corporate privileges of the feudal lords, those held by virtue of their order, and their rights as individual proprietors. Furthermore, the peasantry in the grand duchy of Berg probably gained something more immediate from the abolition without compensation of arbitrary labour services in 1811 [126, 127].

Even if such allowances are made, however, Fehrenbach's overriding conclusion is that the Code was a failure in the states of the Confederation. She attributes this, in part, to Napoleon's ulterior motives, which had more to do with military and fiscal exploitation in the furtherance of his dynastic and social designs than with enlightened principles of legal equality. The result, by 1814 at least, was that the Code had not grown naturally in the German states east of the Rhine but, to use her own simile, had been stunted like a '*Torso*', a trunk without head or limbs. Ironically, it actually did more to entrench the position of the noble lords than to free the peasantry from their sway. Nearly all of those states lacked a dynamic and liberal bourgeoisie, an intermediate class able and ambitious enough to challenge the traditional social and economic role of the old nobility [128].

Perhaps the most striking disparity between Napoleon's advertised plans for reform and their real social and economic effects lay in the kingdom of Westphalia, as Helmut Berding has shown in detail. Created in 1807 as a 'model' state, in part to vindicate the *Code Napoléon* as a reform-manual, its fortunes under Jérôme Bonaparte were much less happy in the event [118]. Following the dispossession of the recalcitrant feudal princes there, the domain lands of the kingdom were reckoned in 1808 to have a capital value of 336 million francs, with a combined income of over 31 million a year. By the middle of 1809 the Imperial land-gifts there numbered 929, out of a total of 4042. Altogether, the income of these Westphalian endowments was around 7 million francs a year, and it rose to some 12 million after the annexation of Hanover early in 1810. The principal *donataires* were Pauline Bonaparte and the military chiefs Berthier, Bernadotte, Lefebvre and Ney, each of whom received *dotations* nominally worth between 100,000 and 180,000 francs a year. A second group of just over 200, again mostly military officers, enjoyed land-gifts ranging from 80,000 down to 10,000 francs each; but the great majority of the Westphalian endowments were much smaller. In December 1810 the richest Hanoverian lands were annexed directly to the Empire [117].

To protect the value of all these *dotations*, as well as of the revenues accruing to Napoleon's *Domaine extraordinaire*, French policy was soon diverted from its initial radical promise. Many former landlords' rights and dues were perpetuated in some way, which in practice undermined the application of the *Code Napoléon* and the principles enshrined in the constitution of the kingdom. Since both the *dotations* and the Imperial domain lands were administered by French agents, they were in effect a state within a state. As such, they were destructive of legal equality and social reform. Berding describes the dichotomy as 'the contradiction between the command to reform and the inhibition on reform' (*der Widerspruch von Reformgebot und Reformverbot*) – in other words between the formal injunction to apply the prescribed principle of legal equality and the practical need to conserve the old social order so as to tap its existing revenues for Imperial use [117: *51*]. This central paradox was never resolved. Berding shows that the social and economic basis of the kingdom of Westphalia was rooted in traditional land relationships. We may safely bury the textbook myth that Jérôme ruled a 'bourgeois monarchy'. The Westphalian endowments were the more easily restored to their former owners by the first Treaty of Paris in 1814.

The work of Monika Senkowska-Gluck and others has established that the duchy of Warsaw also had an increasing importance in Napoleon's spoils system. As a result, the potential of the legal and social reforms inspired there by the French was not fully realised. Attempts to graft the *Code Napoléon* into the social structure of the duchy again strengthened the hold of the old feudal proprietors [136]. Even before the creation of the duchy, Napoleon's decree of 4 June 1807 had ordered a special commission to set aside 20 million francs of capital from the nationalised royal domain lands in Poland. Following his further decrees of 30 June, this sum was to be distributed among twenty-seven French marshals and generals in the form of land-gifts bearing the status of *majorats* under French law, with annual income equivalent to roughly 10 per cent of their capital value. The most important of these was the principality of Lowicz, granted to Davout, with an income of some 200,000 francs a year. Lannes received the principality of Siewierz, with a nominal annual income of 100,000 francs, which passed to his eldest son after the marshal's death in action in 1809. A third beneficiary was Lefebvre, who became the duke of Danzig in recognition of his part in the siege of the city in 1807 [135].

The original twenty-seven endowments in the duchy of Warsaw were to deprive its treasury of something like a fifth of its potential revenue from the nationalised domain lands. The cost of more than 80,000 troops stationed within its borders was another drain on resources, and it faced a serious deficit from the start. The problem was not eased by the territorial accessions (notably Galicia) to the duchy after Austria's defeat in 1809, because at the same time 10 million francs of capital was added to the Imperial endowments there. The latter was distributed mainly to the benefit of Pauline Bonaparte, Masséna, Augereau, Maret, Macdonald, Duroc, Sébastiani, Andréossy and Régnier, and eighteen other *donataires* also received sizable concessions. The real value of these *dotations* had fallen even before the Russian occupation of the duchy, but in any case all were suppressed and reunited with the Crown lands in Poland on 2 May 1813. On 30 May 1814 the French government formally renounced any further claim to them [135].

We may then conclude that from the campaigns of 1805–7 to 1814 Napoleon came increasingly to treat his Italian, German and Polish subjects in ways reminiscent of a warrior-overlord. The ideals of legal equality and the rationalisation of resources were subordinated to his military and fiscal needs, and not least to his dynastic and social designs. Much of the work of 'defeudalisation' or 'modernisation' which has often been claimed for his rule outside France was not consistently implemented. Given the cash incentives also implied, his policies there might – just – be seen as a late variant of 'bastard feudalism', from which the ethic of a reciprocal feudal bond had disappeared, and in which rack-renting for immediate gain had overriden the initial brief of the reforming jurists. The pen in this instance was not mightier than the sword. The result was that feudalism, though abolished in legal principle, actually survived in most of its old forms, such as nobles' privileges, seigneurial dues, serfdom and even labour services. Rather like the enlightened despots before him, Napoleon in effect made his practical compromise with the traditional and tenacious feudal structures of the subject states.

In 1815 the victorious Allies abandoned the compromise and, in Italy, Germany and Poland at any rate, tipped the balance back in favour of the old princes. In spite of his claims to the contrary, or the legend put about after his fall, Napoleon should not be seen as a radical social reformer wherever he intervened. While there is no doubt that his codes spelt the final, definitive, legal extinction of feudalism in France itself, and even by extension in some of the annexed territories, much of the spadework had been done before Brumaire. His 'radicalism' in the subject states was trimmed to serve his military, dynastic and social designs. The old ties of loyalty and habit had been hard to break down. French governors and armies might come and go, but the inertia of the land was resistant to radical change. Part at least of Napoleon's reforms remained more talked about than done. If they really *had* taken root in the subject states of Italy, Germany and Poland, not to mention rebellious Spain, over which the French hold in 1808–14 was at best tenuous, the work of dynastic restoration at the Vienna Congress would certainly have been much more difficult.

6   The Imperial Economy

(i) Agriculture

Research into the economic history of the Napoleonic
period has been active since Louis Bergeron set out
its main themes at the bicentenary conference of 1969,
although agriculture still remains a neglected area much
in need of up-to-date review [142]. The gap is regret-
table, since France in the early nineteenth century was
predominantly an agricultural country, and long remained
so. More than three-quarters of the Empire's GNP, in many
regions appreciably more, derived from agriculture and its
immediately related industries. Most historians are now
agreed that there was little general improvement in agricultural equipment or methods under Napoleon, nothing
at least which might be called an 'agricultural revolution',
notwithstanding the extravagant claims often made by his
officials and some real advances in certain branches. The
economic effects of the Revolutionary land sales, in which
the buyers had often been motivated more by social status
than by the rewards of improved productivity, were similarly conservative. Their retardative influence on French
industrialisation, as well as on the application of capital-
ist methods to agriculture itself, has been noted by many
earlier writers.

On the other hand one can easily forget that Napoleon
was fortunate with his harvests – more fortunate than, say,
the hapless Louis XVI in the 1780s. Only the harvests of
1801–3 and 1811 were widely deficient, and the four-year
cycle from 1806 to 1809 was especially plentiful. This
helps to explain why prices, though generally on an
upward trend, were nevertheless tenable in the critical

food markets for most of the period. Otherwise, an Empire subjected to incessant wars would have suffered far worse price inflation and other pressures on its resources. Agricultural sufficiency not only had a stabilising effect on the mass markets of France, which were essentially local in character; it was also at the heart of popular acquiescence in Napoleon's regime. This, the 'luck factor' so to speak, has not been stressed enough in explanations of his 'pacification' of the peasantry and urban working classes. It may even have been a discouragement to technical improvements in French agriculture at that time. Significantly, when the harvest of 1811 failed in many areas, and when military levies were stepped up in 1812–14, peasant unrest became more widespread. Popular riots also broke out in some towns, prompting a temporary resort to the old price-fixing (*maximum*) of the Revolution.

(ii) Aims of the Continental Blockade

We are rather better informed on the industrial, commercial and financial history of the Empire. This involves the wider repercussions of Napoleon's Continental Blockade, or Continental System as it is often still called [156]. A distinction between the two can and should be made. The *Blockade*, in the strict sense, may be defined as Napoleon's commercial war with Britain, along with its related industrial and financial policies. The *System* subsumed all this but also included the military, political, diplomatic, fiscal, legal and social policies pursued in the 'Grand Empire'. My present concern is with the Blockade. For no doubt understandable reasons, most earlier English writings have concentrated on the maritime aspects of the subject, but in doing so give an unbalanced account of it. Professor F.E. Melvin, for example, thought that 'a study of the diplomacy of the Consulate and Empire furnishes incontrovertible proof that its navigation policy was the dominating element of the Napoleonic regime' [163: *350*]. More recent research into the aims and effects of Napoleon's economic policies on the continental mainland presents a somewhat different picture. The largely dismal fortunes of the beleaguered coastal regions were only part of a much more complex economic experience [154].

It should be said at once that the Continental Blockade of 1806–13 was not an isolated episode but rather the climacteric of a much longer process of maritime conflict and of commercial and industrial rivalry in western Europe. Successive losses of colonial and other transmarine markets and sources of supply had created serious difficulties for France well before Brumaire. In the last years of the old regime, almost a third of her total exports had consisted of colonial re-exports, while a fifth to a quarter of her industrial production had had its outlets in the Antilles and the Spanish colonies. The Atlantic seaboard, and more especially the ports of Bordeaux and Nantes, had then been the most dynamic sector of French trade. As François Crouzet has shown, the wars of the Revolution had steadily undermined that lucrative sector of the French economy, condemning certain home industries to permanent decline, others to prolonged stagnation, and disrupting many of the ancillary industries, trades and financial services [149; 150]. The brief interlude of the Peace of Amiens (March 1802–May 1803), when France regained most of her colonies, did not allow for any sustained recovery in that once buoyant sector of her trade.

The Berlin decree of 21 November 1806 officially declared the British Isles in a state of blockade by land and sea and forbade any communication with them by France or her satellites. This extraordinary measure was justified formally as a response to the British naval blockade of 16 May 1806. In January and November 1807 new orders in council strengthened that blockade and also obliged neutral ships to call at a British port for inspection, to pay duties and seek licences there for trade with enemy ports. Napoleon replied with the Milan decrees of 23 November and 17 December 1807, which in effect extended the embargo on British or British-borne goods to all neutral carriers complying with the orders in council. By then, French maritime trade had again been

96

badly disrupted. The battle of Trafalgar (21 October 1805) signalled the virtual eclipse of the Imperial navy, although its troubles had also set in earlier, and the Boulogne flotilla project of 1803–5 was now in shreds. Thanks to her superior navy and merchant marine, Britain had gained most from the losses of France and her maritime allies.

Against this background of cumulative maritime losses and land-locked power, the Continental Blockade had a dual purpose. Invoking old mercantilist theory, and adapting it crudely to his own military reasoning, Napoleon's first aim was 'to conquer Britain by excess'. His main target was her exports and re-exports; her imports might even be encouraged so long as they were paid for in specie. He assumed that if her industrial products and colonial re-exports were denied outlets in continental Europe, and her bullion reserves were drained away at the same time, inflation would overtake her currency. This would reduce her capacity to finance foreign coalitions against France and force her to sue for an early peace. But, secondly, Napoleon also wanted to create a new system of markets for Imperial manufacturers and merchants on the European mainland. As such, the Blockade was much more than the extended 'coast system' so familiarly recounted in English textbooks. It was, as Albert Sorel remarked long ago, essentially a 'two-trigger engine' (*machine à double détente*): at once a 'war-machine' with destructive intent, set in motion on the land to quarantine the continent from British maritime supremacy, *and* a 'market design' aimed more constructively at establishing French industrial and commercial hegemony on the continental mainland [30]. Napoleon himself boasted at the time that he would 'conquer the sea by mastery of the land'.

In essentials, the twin aims of the original Blockade decrees survived all their later modifications, notably those of 1810. Yet each also had an intrinsic weakness. In the first case, Napoleon lacked the naval means to direct his 'war-machine' against Britain directly on the seas. His 'Continental Blockade' was therefore something of a misnomer, being in effect a 'self-blockade', a *boycott* of British goods imposed on Imperial subjects by their own government. Born of military victory, its implementation was inconceivable without the continuing superiority of French land power. In the second case, the French market design rested on the over-optimistic assumption that the Empire could be economically self-sufficient on the continental mainland and also oblige her client states to draw on that sufficiency for their own needs. If France could not yet replace Britain as 'the workshop of the world', she might at least aspire to become 'the workshop of Europe', or as it were the 'Grand Provisioner' of the 'Grand Empire'. This vision was necessarily conceived in the longer view, once British trade had been banished from the scene.

Even in its more positive form, however, the Blockade was never allowed to work equitably. The French continental market design created an artificial hothouse atmosphere in which the native growths of industry and trade could not thrive by natural intercourse with the wider world. In a letter to Eugène de Beauharnais on 23 August 1810 Napoleon spelt out the inflexible principle of 'France first' (*la France avant tout*). It was to be strictly applied to those who, in Italy and Germany especially, lay beyond the Imperial frontiers. Napoleon might just conceivably have aimed for a continental 'common market', and in doing so have given his client states an incentive to sever their ties with Britain in return for reciprocal trading rights in the large French market. Instead, he fiercely upheld the old mercantilist doctrine of full protection for the home industries and also imposed one-sided preferential trade tariffs on several of the subject states. This was in effect the formula for an 'uncommon market', or what Louis Bergeron has called 'a kind of "one-way common market," in which imposed commercial treaties and unilateral decisions produced an exchange system in the interests of France alone' [16: *173*]. Its motto might well have been: 'BUY FRENCH!' Just as Napoleon wanted political and military vassals rather than independent partners, so he sought economic dependencies and tributaries, not competitive allies. For the client states, indeed for many home consumers too, the whole design came to be seen as a contrivance by which the higher French cost of living could be thrust on the Continent at large. Its 'sacred egoism' was transparent and ultimately proved self-defeating.

The Imperial decrees of 10 June 1806 and 10 October 1810, for example, officially declared that the Kingdom of Italy was to be a sort of 'reserved market' for whole categories of French goods. They unilaterally outlawed traditional trading links between the kingdom and foreign countries, such as Switzerland, and threatened old commercial ties within Italy itself [165]. Germany, with its vast hinterland and multiple land frontiers, could not be quarantined from foreign competition in the same way. Napoleon made no comparable attempt to 'reserve' her markets, partly because the transit routes there were crucial to French trade with the Baltic, Poland, and thence to Russia, and depended on a whole relay of international services. On the other hand, as the French trade missions of 1807–11 made clear, he wished to turn his military hegemony in Germany to economic advantage as well. In particular, he encouraged Imperial manufacturers and merchants to exploit the town fairs of Frankfurt am Main and Leipzig, then still the major events of the commercial calendar in central and northern Germany [154].

(iii) Effects of Napoleon's economic policies

The trouble with Napoleon's economic reasoning was that it presupposed a watertight Blockade, a populace willing to buy foodstuffs, industrial primary materials and manufactured goods at the appreciably higher French prices, and an efficient customs service. In all those respects the results did not match the plan. The Blockade was never fully effective. Its military apparatus, for a start, was depleted during hostilities on the Continent, when the troops were needed for combat. The dreaded *douaniers* who manned its civilian arm were universally disliked, and many proved to be corrupt. So did a number of French generals charged with customs surveillance, since the spoils of contraband traffic were often very tempting. British smugglers were adept at beating the Blockade, taking advantage of osmotic inlets in Holland, along the North Sea and Baltic coasts, in the Iberian peninsula and later Italy. Imperial subjects connived with profiteers to bring in prohibited goods.

Smuggling might even be seen as the most ubiquitous form of popular disobedience to Imperial rule. Napoleon himself implicitly recognised this in his issues of special licences for trade with the enemy. The latter were regarded at first as *ad hoc* concessions to relieve the glutted wine and grain stocks of the Atlantic littoral [147]. On one celebrated occasion, when her harvest failed in 1810, Britain was ironically let off the hook by large shipments of grain under licence from the west country of France [155]. Seeing its fiscal potential, Napoleon regularised the issue of licences by his Saint-Cloud decree of 3 July 1810. Their multiplication in 1813, when he was in more desperate need of cash, made nonsense of the official embargoes.

In all, the economic effects of the Blockade and its continental market design were far from uniform. Important regional, sectoral and chronological distinctions have to be made. The maritime ports and their dependent hinterlands not surprisingly suffered most from the loss of sea-borne trade and from the British naval blockades. Ancillary industries like shipbuilding, rope-making, sailcloth manufacture, tobacco processing and sugar refining languished in their turn. If woollens recovered under Napoleon from their earlier setbacks, the decline of the traditional linen industries of the Nord, the Aisne and the western regions of France, already well in evidence during the Revolutionary wars, was further accentuated. Based on increasingly obsolete methods, they had no real capacity for technical conversion, and for many the loss of overseas markets proved a lethal blow.

All those setbacks were most keenly felt, as they had been during the later 1790s, along the Channel and Atlantic seaboard of France. And yet, as Paul Butel found in Bordeaux, some essential commercial functions were kept going under neutral (chiefly American) flags and by the coasting trade until about 1807, when a more profound crisis overtook the port [145, 146]. There, and elsewhere, capital investment tended to desert the trading sector and take refuge in land. The old merchant oligarchy of Nantes, for instance, also found some minor compensations in the coasting trade, but generally it suffered a diminution of wealth and social status. Its slave trade, once so lucrative, had withered steadily after the revolt and loss of Santo Domingo in 1791 [158]. The Marseillais were better placed to risk expeditions to North Africa, Italy and particularly Spain, but 1808 again seems to have marked the start of a prolonged decline [162]. It is true that Marseilles found a new role as a regional centre of distribution, taking advantage of traffic in the Rhône corridor, but its crucial Mediterranean exchanges did not revive before the favourable franchise granted under the Restoration. As older mercantile houses foundered, the way was opened for a breed of 'new men', risen opportunists, to amass quick fortunes through sly speculations in military and naval supplies, grain, wines, colonial goods and contraband. Some had bought *biens nationaux* during the Revolution, and under Napoleon their names often appeared on the lists of the departmental *notables*, an official sign of their social ascent.

The great majority of continental people, however, did not live in the maritime ports. Their traditional economic orbits were otherwise orientated, and their experience of the Blockade was altogether more oblique. While their staple agricultural activities served scattered local markets more or less immune from the fluctuations of international trade, their more dynamic industrial and commercial sectors certainly had wider continental horizons. On the French mainland, formal protection from British competition in the home market and favourable opportunities for export to clients across the Alps and the Rhine, or via the German transit routes to parts further afield, had some positive effect. As the sea lanes were progressively closed to Imperial shipping, so the reorientation of trade routes increased the relative importance of inland centres like Paris (for luxury goods, fashion ware, colonial products, and the new genre of cottons) and Lyons (for silkstuffs). It also gave a fillip to entrepôts on the eastern frontier, most notably Strasbourg, which may have handled as much as a third of the Empire's export and import trade during the Blockade. The city's legitimate Rhine traffic alone doubled and in certain peak periods even quadrupled in volume by comparison with the annual average before 1806, and the additional spoils of its flourishing contraband dealings were considerable. The transit trade in wines, spirits, other agricultural products, cottons, silkstuffs (for which the Imperial Court was also a major client) and some metallurgical products was active during the years from Tilsit to the late summer of 1810 [154].

The figures cited by Maurice Lévy-Leboyer, for instance, suggest that French consumption of raw cotton, though far short of the British levels, roughly doubled between 1803 and 1807 when compared with 1802. They rose again to a peak in 1810, before falling appreciably during the late Empire [161: *30*]. A shortfall in colonial supplies could thus be made up in part by increased shipments overland from the Levant, which until 1811 entered the Empire mainly through Strasbourg. These were prone to prolonged delays during hostilities, however, and I am much more sceptical about Lévy-Leboyer's further claim that 'French' [read 'Imperial'?] exports of cotton goods increased tenfold in the period 1807–10 [161: *55*]. In any event, the benefits of expanded production in textiles were not confined to France; they extended to the annexed lands in Belgium, where Ghent was particularly prominent, and on the German left bank of the Rhine [152]. During preparations for major campaigns, the war industries also received the boost of increased orders. In some areas the military market for woollens as well as for armaments and other field supplies held the key to local production.

Industrial expansion encouraged some technical improvements, again chiefly in the mechanisation of the cotton industries, and more especially spinning, although the main advances here were to come after 1815. Under Napoleon, the new machines were usually hybrid imitations of older English models, the so-called 'mule-jennies' most notably, some of which indeed were installed and worked by British émigrés [157]. On the other hand, such machines had a significant impact on productivity only in the larger enterprises, like those of Richard-Lenoir in Paris, Liévin Bauwens at Passy and Ghent, and in the important concentrations of spinning works in the Seine-Inférieure, Eure and Nord. In the Haut-Rhin (upper Alsace), spinning and the less mechanised branch of weaving were feeder industries for the critical sector of calico-printing, above all in Mulhouse. Paradoxically, the very success of the cotton industries made life harder for the manufacturers of linens and hemp in the endless search for markets. In most areas, the textile industries remained essentially artisanal and even domestic in structure, widely dependent as in weaving on the putting-out system, and geared to undynamic local markets. In times before the railways, road and water transport had obvious limitations, seasonal in part, and could not fully replace the bulk carriage by sea which had been lost.

The progress of the chemical industry was often linked with the relative buoyancy of textiles, for instance in developing artificial dyestuffs and bleaching materials, and with the rather less active metallurgical sector. It drew on the distinguished tradition of French science and was represented under the Empire by such celebrated *savants* as Berthollet and Chaptal. Some of the experiments with acids eventually had industrial application, while those with artificial soda (based on the Leblanc process earlier) were widely taken up by the soap manufacturers of Marseilles [166]. The iron industry, by contrast, stuck to older methods, almost everywhere preferring charcoal to coal for smelting. Larger enterprises like those at Hayange and Le Creusot, where smelting by coke was known, were in any case foundations of the old regime. One of the most active mining and iron-producing zones of the Empire lay outside France, in Walloon Belgium, where woollens also did well [153]. Of the 'new industries' intended to replace colonial products in French consumption, only beet-sugar made much headway, but late in the Empire and with an uncertain future.

The heyday of the Empire's inland economic expansion can be dated to 1807–10, but new troubles then intervened. The economic crisis of 1810–11 was part of a wider international haemorrhage, whose origins lay not least in Britain, where panic and depression had set in after the trade boom of 1809 [148]. Its continental repercussions soon extended to Hamburg, Bremen, Amsterdam, Rotterdam, Paris, Lyons, Strasbourg and the Swiss financial centres. The crisis in the French Empire itself first hit the banking and dependent commercial houses during the last quarter of 1810, as old debts were called in and new credit was frozen, and then settled on the industrial sector during the first half of 1811 [167]. Those ructions were further complicated by monetary disorders, evident even earlier, which lingered on till 1813 in some regions. Arising from debasements of the currency and exacerbated by speculation, the monetary crisis led to a general scarcity of specie [65].

Taken as a whole, the French crisis cannot be attributed wholly or even directly to the Blockade. In its financial and commercial phase it had more to do with speculative over-stocking. As foreign outlets suddenly defaulted, the wine trade and colonial goods sector could not dispose of their surpluses. In its industrial phase the crisis was paradoxically also one of glut, of over- rather than under-production, and here too of faltering markets. The problem lay in demand, not in the technical capacity to supply. As such, it immediately affected the silk industries of the Lyonnais [160]. The more mechanised cotton industries suffered even more, since these depended on a rapid turnover and ready credit and often lacked enough capital to survive the squeeze on their liquidity. 'Ploughed-back profits', or *autofinancement*, was of no use when the profits themselves evaporated. Some of the foremost victims were large houses specialising in cottons, such as Gros-Davillier of Paris, whose near bankruptcy early in 1811 seriously embarrassed its sister house at Wesserling in Alsace. It had to be rescued by massive government loans, but many lesser firms which lacked that life-line sank under the 'cascade of bankruptcies' [144].

Napoleon's modification of the Blockade by the Trianon tariff of 5 August and the Fontainebleau decree of 18 October 1810 was not directly due to the crisis, since those measures actually preceded the worst of its disruptions. He seems here to have been motivated more by a contradictory mixture of fiscal need and a new resolve to tighten customs surveillance. The Trianon tariff allowed the import of many colonial goods hitherto prohibited, but subjected them to exorbitant duties. The Fontainebleau decree toughened the Blockade against British manufactured goods and intensified the so-called 'customs terror' (*terreur douanière*) of 1810–12 in the North Sea ports, especially at Hamburg and Bremen. But even if they were not the immediate cause of the crisis, the new measures unquestionably exacerbated its effects in many areas. The expansionary momentum of 1807–10 was lost; what followed was slow and hard-won recovery during the latter half of 1811 and in 1812, when military reverses brought further economic upsets.

One detail of the crisis and its aftermath, so far only sketchily treated in secondary works, clearly merits more detailed research along the lines attempted by Max Tacel for Italy [164]. It is the impact of Napoleon's economic policies on the agriculture of the subject states and their related effects on Imperial export markets there. The French Empire was a large free-trade zone, which is why the partial harvest failure of 1811 could be eased by the shipment of grain from the least to the most affected regions. In good years, however, the Empire could not absorb the agricultural surpluses of its client states, since it already had enough of its own. At the same time the Blockade officially forbade the disposal of such surpluses through British trade or through neutrals obeying the orders in council. The depressing effect on agricultural prices in the client states weakened their purchasing power, that is their capacity to absorb French goods, so that Imperial exporters felt the pinch in their turn.

This, it seems, was the most harmful effect of Napoleon's economic policies on the agricultural regions of the 'Grand Empire' formerly reliant on maritime outlets. Its repercussions reached from the Baltic to the Mediterranean. One might add here that certain of the most capable industrial competitors of France were similarly placed on the losing side of the Empire's customs frontiers and felt the chill draught of exclusion from its markets. If the textile manufacturers of the grand duchy of Berg (which included the

Ruhrland) were perhaps most disadvantaged, especially after 1810, their Swiss counterparts also suffered from the official closure of traditional outlets in France and Italy [134]. The main beneficiary of the Blockade beyond the Imperial frontiers was the cotton industry of Saxony, whose production increased impressively, but it was far from being a typical case [156].

The Blockade finally disintegrated in 1813, when military and fiscal exactions in the defence of the Empire imposed even greater strains, and when hostilities cut across the inland trade routes. Measured statistically, its overall record did not justify the great hopes of 1806. While the official values of French exports to the German and Italian states generally held up well in the years 1806–12, and at an appreciably higher level than earlier, the maritime sector was further undermined. It was not until 1826 that the *total* value of French foreign trade again reached the level of 1787 [154: *285–9*]. In this sense one may say that the cumulative effects of her transmarine losses during the Revolutionary and Napoleonic wars cost France nearly forty years of normal commercial growth.

So, too, the map of French industry in 1815 looked rather different from that of 1793. Commenting on the long-term effects of the maritime wars and of the Blockade, François Crouzet goes so far as to speak of a 'shift of industry from the seaboard to the heartland of western Europe', so marked by 1814 that 'the axis of the Continental economy had now moved from the Atlantic toward the Rhine' [150: *586–7*]. Louis Bergeron argues similarly that the inland thrust of Napoleon's policies was to 'reorganise by force' what he calls 'the political and economic space on both sides of the Rhine' [143: *552*]. But Britain, conversely, could not be stopped from engrossing the markets of the wider world. Her global superiority over France in naval, commercial, financial and industrial power, as well as in technological skills, was greater in 1815 than it had been in 1793, and long remained so [151]. The Continental Blockade was by no means solely responsible for this, but later free traders often cited it as a classic example of the futility of commercial embargoes and of the autarkist myth.

7 The Legacy

If the military turning-point in Napoleon's fortunes was the disastrous Russian campaign of 1812, while the position of his forces in the Peninsula also worsened during 1813, it nevertheless took all the allies of the Sixth Coalition to bring him down in the campaigns of 1813–14. In that victory the contribution of Russia was probably the decisive factor, helped no doubt by Prussian mobilisation early in 1813. For if Britain provided most of the lubrication of the Coalition, thanks to the heavy subsidies Castlereagh was able to extract from parliament [173], Tsar Alexander I provided the resolute will to pursue and destroy the emperor while he was in retreat. It was his *Drang nach Westen*, as it were, almost a spiritual crusade, that eventually gave the Allies their superiority over the French and inspired his vision of a Holy Alliance at the peace. In spite of Napoleon's desperate and often brilliant efforts during the campaigns of 1813–14, he was forced to abdicate on 6 April 1814. The claims made on behalf of the King of Rome, the presumptive Napoleon II, with Marie-Louise as regent, had also foundered in the final 'betrayal', and the restoration of Louis XVIII was agreed [171].

The extraordinary episode of the Hundred Days (20 March–22 June 1815), though dramatically revealing of how puny men will respond to the fear of great ones, brought no lasting initiatives in the temporarily restored Imperial framework. It is unlikely that Benjamin Constant's 'Additional Act to the Constitutions of the Empire' (23 April), a pseudo-liberalising gesture to rally bourgeois support to the regime, would have been honoured by Napoleon if Waterloo had turned out differently. As the high incidence of abstentions in the plebiscite on

107

the Act suggested, the propertied classes, the base of the former Imperial élite, were already hedging their bets and vindicating the old axiom that discretion is the better part of valour [169]. The most spontaneous rally in fact occurred among the incumbent personnel of some provincial towns like Rennes and Dijon and among the working people of certain Paris sections. These so-called 'federations' for the defence of the Empire in 1815 certainly bore witness to 'popular Bonapartism' in action, but they lacked the necessary military muscle and organisation and were also ideologically divided among themselves [168]. After Waterloo (18 June 1815) the statesmen assembled in Vienna were taking no chances. Napoleon's second abdication on 22 June marked the end of his rule, if also the start of his legend so grandiloquently cultivated by Las Cases and others during the years of exile on St Helena (1815–21) and by later Bonapartist cults [170].

The summer of 1815 is, then, the point at which we can take stock of what Napoleon's rule had ultimately achieved, and what it had cost. The territorial upshot was no worse than might have been expected after the Hundred Days. France would have fared better if Napoleon had accepted peace terms early. In the event the first Treaty of Paris (30 May 1814) gave the Bourbons the frontiers of 1792, which included Avignon, the Comtat Venaissin, and parts of Belgium, the Rhenish left bank and Savoy. Apart from St Lucia, Tobago and Mauritius, all the captured French colonies were restored by Britain. The second Peace of Paris (20 November 1815), which was duly incorporated in the final Vienna Settlement, cut France back to her frontiers of 1789, but allowed her to keep Avignon and the Venaissin, Mulhouse in upper Alsace, and indeed nearly the whole of Alsace-Lorraine. If la gloire had been a powerful motive in Napoleon's ambition, 1815 brought the French back to a more mundane reality. In the first instance this took the form of a war indemnity of 700 million francs, due within five years, plus the occupation and upkeep of 150,000 Allied troops on the northern and eastern frontiers until it was paid.

What, next, of the human cost? Estimates have varied

enormously over the past century and a half, but the present consensus puts the war losses in the land armies under the Empire at around 916,000 within the 89 departments which remained French in 1815, out of a total of some 1.4 million for the whole period 1792–1814. These figures include those killed in action, the much larger numbers who subsequently died of their wounds or from illness, the victims of exhaustion or exposure to the cold, and prisoners of war not later accounted for [97]. A great many others were permanently invalided. Since the war dead fell largely within the most fertile age-groups, particularly in 1812–14, it is tempting to link them in some way with the markedly slower growth-rate of the French population, when compared with others, throughout the nineteenth century. But this now seems too facile. The fall in the birth-rate had begun during the Revolution, for reasons not always directly linked with war losses. Furthermore, the wars of the Empire appear to have boosted nuptiality in France, on a particularly rising curve in 1809–13, as potential recruits married to avoid conscription. The result was not necessarily a higher incidence of births, since there is also evidence of a long-term trend towards smaller families, which itself may chiefly reflect a psychological adjustment to the Revolutionary laws on property inheritance (*partage*) [16: *110–14*].

On the other hand, the loss of so many men certainly upset the population balance between the sexes in France, no doubt denying many thousands of eligible young women the chance of marital procreation. In the long term, the effect must have been to reduce the number of births that might otherwise have occurred. Napoleon is reported to have dismissed the carnage of bloody battles in a phrase borrowed (perhaps via Mirabeau) from the great Condé on the evening of Séneffe (1674): 'one Paris night will replace them all' (*une nuit de Paris remplacera cela*). Taken literally, this informal inducement to promiscuous patriotism was of course fanciful nonsense. Births in Paris in the early nineteenth century averaged between 25,000 and 30,000 a year. On such a performance, even the most passionate Paris night could scarcely have produced 100 new recruits [97]!

The grandeur of the Imperial nobility and social promotions lived on mostly in the Napoleonic legend, but it was to revive in more practical forms, though with important modifications, during the Second Empire of Napoleon III (1852–70). Under the Restoration, the former Imperial nobles were held in some disdain by the old nobility, and their titles had no secure legal status. The surviving marshals, with the exception of Davout, received the Grand Cross of the Order of Saint-Louis, but only Victor, Oudinot, Marmont, Macdonald and Saint-Cyr (who became Louis XVIII's minister of war) found any real favour with the Bourbons. The other top brass of the Imperial army, where it continued in the profession, had to truckle to the authority of the émigré commanders who had returned with Louis XVIII. On the other hand, Napoleon left an important legacy to French society in his consolidation of the Revolutionary land settlement. Landownership continued to be the first measure of social pre-eminence in France for many decades after 1815. If the former Imperial *notables* were often overshadowed by the old nobility as landowners and taxpayers during the Restoration, and thus had a less prominent public role among the élite of its 'legal nation', they tenaciously defended their earlier material gains.

In the subject states, however, Napoleon's legal and social reforms seem in the end to have had much less impact on the old landowning élites and feudal structures, not least because his use of their resources to fuel his Imperial spoils system undermined the implementation of his codes. His political legacy across the Alps and the Rhine lived on after 1815 in several ways, although his impact on the official map and institutions of Germany was the more substantial. The old Holy Roman Empire had gone, once and for all. The German Confederation (*Bund*) of 1815, which at first brought together thirty-eight states, marked important territorial and institutional changes from the political fragmentation of some hundreds of small states (*Kleinstaaterei*) of the eighteenth century. By contrast, the legitimist principle upheld at the Vienna Congress ensured that the political map of Italy in 1815 looked rather more like that of 1789. Yet in both countries the experience of French rule, not least the vision

of a greater political union and the lessons of more professional bureaucratic structures, was to influence nationalist
and liberal ideologies of reform alike. If the Church lands
in Italy were restored to the Pope in 1815, the clerical confiscations and other forms of secularisation in many parts
of Germany were not reversed. In all, it would be fair to
call this Napoleon's legacy of 'rationalisation' if not 'modernisation' beyond the frontiers of France, but even so the
social (and particularly the aristocratic) restraints on such
processes remained endemic in both Italy and Germany.

The economic balance-sheet is mixed but on the
whole negative, although Napoleon himself cannot be held
accountable for the cumulative losses of the long maritime
wars. His Continental Blockade might even be seen as a last
resort, without alternative, as an extraordinary contrivance
born of war, of economic *dis*location, which would have been
unthinkable in a peacetime context. Yet just as it failed
to destroy the British economy and force an early peace,
so the ultimate collapse of the French continental market
design is also clear. Louis XVIII resorted to protectionist
tariffs almost at once. The most enduring effect of the
maritime wars and of the Blockade was the reorientation of French industrial and commercial growth away
from the Atlantic seaboard towards the inland regions.
This economic shift gave a particular importance to the
north-eastern departments of France, but the south-west
was destined to become one of her more under-developed
regions. Belgium, which had been among the most industrially advanced and advantaged territories under French
rule, passed from France to the crown of Holland at the
peace settlement and was not to gain independence until
1831. Her loss of open access to French markets during
that interlude was a painful wrench. The industries of the
Rhenish left bank which came under Prussian rule in 1815
faced similar difficulties of readjustment.

What, then, positively survived the collapse of the
Empire in France? The short answer is: the legal codes
and much of their judicial infrastructure, the prefectures,
the financial and fiscal reforms (including not least the Bank
of France), the Concordat, and the *lycées*. Such institutional

achievements did not stem from the battle-field, which adds some weight to the view that Napoleon did more than most of the great military 'dictators' of history to *civilise* his legacy. The last question, whether or not his impact was ultimately more constructive or destructive for France and for Europe, depends on one's ideological and even moral assumptions. For those who valued strong government and the grandeur of France, the legacy of the First Empire was powerfully evocative.

The source and motive force of this legacy lay in Napoleon's charisma, which is also one of the most difficult facets of his career to pin down precisely in analytical terms. In a perceptive essay which offers a useful synopsis of his earlier work on the formation of Napoleon's personality, Harold T. Parker identifies at least six elements 'interplaying in Bonaparte's consciousness': his desire to be first and master of all situations; the noble officer ethic of glory ('a dazzling fame') and honour; his youthful enthusiasm for historical characters who (for him) personified masterly qualities; his own brilliant victories and civil achievements which could be related to such characters; the opportunity to match such examples of past renown in the eyes of his own and of future audiences; and his inner, compelling feeling of being a man of destiny and of good fortune. 'From this interplay', Professor Parker concludes, 'emerged the basic controlling self-image of an authoritative military-civilian ruler of contemporary and historical renown', which recalls Napoleon's own belief that 'I am of the race that founds empires' [172: 456–7].

Such ambitions infused most of his actions: his military achievements, the creation of such institutions as the Legion of Honour and the Imperial nobility, his vast official and private correspondence, and his many personal reminiscences to those who later formed his – literally – captive audience. The acclamation of fame, honour and grandeur was even given a quasi-divine sanction, for instance in the Imperial Catechism and in the celebration of 'Saint Napoleon's Day' (15 August) in place of the traditional Feast of the Assumption, both instituted in 1806. The victory of Austerlitz was thereafter celebrated officially each year by a

Te Deum in many churches on the first Sunday of December. Some of the best-known monuments of Paris today, such as the Arc de Triomphe de l'Étoile and the Arc du Carrousel, bear witness to the Napoleonic triumphalism in which they were originally conceived.

Liberals, socialists and pacifists have seen it all rather differently, however. For them, the terrible human cost, the physical despoliation of conquered territories, the humiliation of proud peoples, and the curtailment of the right to act, speak and publish freely could not be justified by the institutional reforms, orderly government, and the passing experience of Imperial glory. Yet the difficulty with so many of their harsher verdicts on Napoleon is that they judge him not according to the values of his own day but to those of later times. They have sometimes failed to appreciate that, in spite of his great military and political power, he was neither omniscient nor a wholly free agent. Much of his inheritance had limited his options and tied his hands from the start. The sea and all its riches, most obviously, were practically closed to him. In assessing his record in civil rights, in intellectual freedom, in humanitarian endeavour, in social improvement, or in economic growth – all consuming objects of our own age – one should remember that he was a soldier by training and ruled a state almost constantly at war. The Napoleonic legend would not have survived as long as it did if something of the Imperial charisma had not taken root in the hearts of many subjects. For them at least, the legacy of the Empire was positive, and Napoleon's place in the pantheon of French patriotism second to none.

Appendix I: Dynasty, Nobility and *Notables* of the Napoleonic Empire

Napoleon

Emperor of the French, King of Italy, Mediator of the Swiss Confederation, Protector of the Confederation of the Rhine, etc.

Princes of the first order: members of or those related by marriage to the Imperial family who became satellite kings: *Joseph*, king of Naples (March 1806) and then of Spain (June 1808); *Louis*, king of Holland (June 1806–July 1810); *Jérôme*, king of Westphalia (July 1807); *Joachim Murat* (m. Caroline Bonaparte), grand duke of Berg (March 1806) and king of Naples (July 1808)

Princes(ses) of the second order: *Élisa Bonaparte* (m. Félix Bacciochi), princess of Piombino (1805) and of Lucca (1806), grand duchess of Tuscany (1809); *Eugène de Beauharnais*, viceroy of Italy (June 1805); *Berthier*, prince of Neuchâtel (March 1806) and of Wagram (December 1809)

Princes of the third order: *Talleyrand*, prince of Benevento (June 1806); *Bernadotte*, prince of Ponte Corvo (June 1806) [crown prince of Sweden, October 1810]

The 22 recipients of the 'ducal grand-fiefs of the Empire' created in March 1806 from conquered lands around Venice, in the kingdom of Naples, in Massa-Carrara, Parma and Piacenza. Similar endowments were later made from the conquered lands which formed the duchy of Warsaw (July 1807)

These were granted to Napoleon's top military commanders, including most of the marshals, or to members of his family, and were convertible into hereditary estates (*majorats*)

The dukes, counts, barons and chevaliers of the Empire created after the March decrees of 1808, and who together probably numbered around 3600 by 1814

These included high-ranking officers, ministers, councillors of state, senators, legislators, archbishops, bishops, prefects, presidents of departmental electoral colleges, of the civil, criminal and appeal courts, mayors of large cities, officers of the Legion of Honour, some academics and artists

The mass of lesser military and civilian beneficiaries (*donataires*) of Imperial land-gifts (*dotations*), of whom there were nearly 6000 by 1814; and the members of the Legion of Honour, whose number by then had risen to over 32,000

All the remaining *notables* of the 130 Imperial departments: sub-prefects, mayors, other officials of the administrative, judicial and educational services of the state, members of the departmental councils, of the electoral colleges, and of the various chambers of commerce, etc. (a total of perhaps 100,000)

Appendix II: List of the Chief Appointments and Honours Bestowed by Napoleon

(An asterisk denotes the names of the marshals)

Arrighi	Duke of Padua (1808).
*Augereau	Marshal (1804). Duke of Castiglione (1808).
Bacciochi	Prince of Piombino (1805) and of Lucca (1806) [cf. Bonaparte, Élisa, below].
Barbé-Marbois	Minister of the treasury (1801-6). President of the court of accounts (1807–14). Count (1813).
Beauharnais, Eugène de	Viceroy of Italy (1805–14). Arch-Chancellor of state.
*Bernadotte	Marshal (1804). Prince of Ponte Corvo (1806).
*Berthier	Marshal (1804). Prince of Neuchâtel (1806). Prince of Wagram (1809). Chief of staff (1796–1814). Minister of war (1799–1800, 1800–7). Vice-Constable of the Empire.
*Bessières	Marshal (1804). Duke of Istria (1809). Commander of the Imperial Guard.
Bigot de Préameneu	Minister of ecclesiastical affairs (1808–14). Count (1808).
Bonaparte, Caroline	Grand duchess of Berg (1806–8). Queen of Naples (1808–15) [cf. Murat, below].
Bonaparte, Élisa	Princess of Piombino (1805) and of Lucca (1806) [cf. Bacciochi, above]. Grand duchess of Tuscany (1809).
Bonaparte, Jérôme	King of Westphalia (1807–13).
Bonaparte, Joseph	King of Naples (1806–8). King of Spain (1808–13). Grand Elector of the Empire.

115

Bonaparte, Louis	King of Holland (1806–10). High Constable of the Empire.
Bonaparte, Pauline	Duchess of Guastalla (1806) [cf. Borghese, below].
Borghese, Prince	Duke of Guastalla (1806). Governor General of the departments beyond the Alps.
*Brune	Marshal (1804).
Cambacérès	Arch-Chancellor of the Empire. Duke of Parma (1808).
Caulaincourt	Duke of Vicenza (1808). Grand master of the horse (1804). Ambassador to Russia (1807–11). Minister of foreign affairs (1813–14, 1815).
Champagny	Duke of Cadore (1809). Minister of the interior (1804–7) and of foreign affairs (1807–11).
Chaptal	Minister of the interior (1800–4). Count (1808). Count of Chanteloup, with its *majorat* (1810).
Clarke	Duke of Feltre (1809). Minister of war (1807–14).
Crétet	Governor of the Bank of France (1806). Minister of the interior (1807–9). Count of Champmol (1808).
Daru	Intendant general of the Grand Army and of the conquered territories (1805). Count (1809). Minister secretary of state (1811–13). Minister of war administration (1813–14, 1815).
*Davout	Marshal (1804). Duke of Auerstädt (1808). Prince of Eckmühl (1809).
Decrès	Minister of the navy (1801–14). Vice-admiral (1804). Count (1808). Duke (1813).
Dejean	Minister of war administration (1802–9). Count (1808). Grand chancellor of the Legion of Honour (1815).
Duroc	Grand marshal of the palace. Duke of Friuli (1808).
Fesch, Cardinal	Grand almoner. Archbishop of Lyons.
Fouché	Duke of Otranto (1809). Minister of general police (1799–1802, 1804–10).
Gaudin	Duke of Gaëta (1809). Minister of finances (1799–1814, 1815).
Girard	Duke of Ligny (1815).
*Gouvion Saint-Cyr	Marshal (1812). Count (1808).
*Grouchy	Marshal (1815). Count (1809).
*Jourdan	Marshal (1804).
Junot	Duke of Abrantès (1809).
*Kellermann	Honorary marshal (1804). Duke of Valmy (1808).
Lacuée	Count of Cessac (1808). Minister of war administration (1809–13).

*Lannes	Marshal (1804). Duke of Montebello (1808).
Lebrun	Arch-Treasurer of the Empire and Governor General of the Dutch departments. Duke of Piacenza (1808).
*Lefebvre	Honorary marshal (1804). Duke of Danzig (1807).
*Macdonald	Marshal (1809). Duke of Taranto (1808).
Maret	Duke of Bassano (1809). Secretary general (1799–1804) and then minister secretary of state (1804–11, 1813–14, 1815). Minister of foreign affairs (1811–13).
*Marmont	Marshal (1809). Duke of Ragusa (1808).
*Masséna	Marshal (1804). Duke of Rivoli (1808). Prince of Essling (1810).
Melzi d'Eril	Duke of Lodi (1807). Chancellor of the Kingdom of Italy.
Mollien	Minister of the treasury (1806–14, 1815). Count (1808).
*Moncey	Marshal (1804). Duke of Conegliano (1808).
Montalivet	Minister of the interior (1809–14). Count (1808).
*Mortier	Marshal (1804). Duke of Treviso (1808).
*Murat	Marshal (1804). Military governor of Paris (1804). Grand duke of Berg (1806–8). King of Naples (1808–15). Grand Admiral of the Empire.
*Ney	Marshal (1804). Duke of Elchingen (1808). Prince of the Moskwa (1813).
*Oudinot	Marshal (1809). Duke of Reggio (1810).
*Pérignon	Honorary marshal (1804). Count (1811).
*Poniatowski, Prince	Marshal (1813). Minister of war in the duchy of Warsaw (1807).
Portalis	Minister of ecclesiastical affairs (1804–7).
Régnier	Duke of Massa (1809). Minister of justice (1802–13).
Roullet de la Bouillerie	Receiver-general of the Grand Army. Treasurer-general of the *Domaine extraordinaire* (1810).
Savary	Duke of Rovigo (1808). Minister of general police (1810–14).
*Sérurier	Honorary marshal (1804). Count (1808).
*Soult	Marshal (1804). Duke of Dalmatia (1808).
*Suchet	Marshal (1811). Duke of Albufera (1813).
Talleyrand-Périgord	Prince of Benevento (1806). Minister of foreign affairs (1799–1807). Vice-Grand Elector of the Empire.
*Victor	Marshal (1807). Duke of Belluno (1808).

117

Appendix III: The Ten 'Grand Dignitaries' of the Empire

Grand Elector	Joseph Bonaparte, king of Naples and then of Spain
Vice-Grand Elector	Talleyrand, prince of Benevento
High Constable	Louis Bonaparte, king of Holland
Vice-Constable	Berthier, prince of Neuchâtel and of Wagram
Arch-Chancellor	Cambacérès, duke of Parma
Arch-Treasurer Governor General of the Dutch departments }	Lebrun, duke of Piacenza
Grand Admiral	Murat, grand duke of Berg and then king of Naples
Arch-Chancellor of State	Eugène de Beauharnais, viceroy of Italy
Governor General of the departments beyond the Alps	Prince Camillo Borghese, duke of Guastalla

The departments of the French Republic after the creation
of the Napoleonic prefectures in 1800

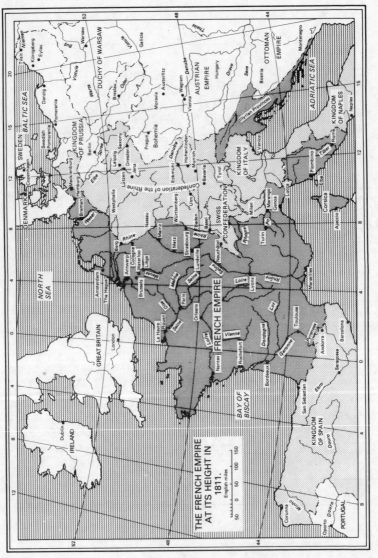

The French Empire at its height in 1811

Glossary

agrégation: qualification reinstated in 1808 for the recruitment of teachers in state schools.

anoblis: those who, of commoner birth under the old regime, were ennobled either through the purchase of office bestowing nobility or otherwise by royal writ.

arrêté: decision, order or decree of the government.

assignats: paper money of the Revolution (1789–96), notionally secured on anticipated receipts from the sale of the national lands (*biens nationaux*).

Auditeurs au Conseil d'état: a new and exemplary corps of professional officials formed in 1803 and attached to the council of state.

biens nationaux: lands confiscated during the Revolution, at first from the Church and Crown, later from the émigrés, suspects and condemned persons, and taken into 'national' (i.e. state) ownership for eventual sale to private buyers (*acquéreurs*).

Brumaire: the month of the Republican calendar in which, on 18th–19th of the Year VIII (9–10 November 1799), Napoleon's *coup d'état* overthrew the Directory.

cadastre: land survey used for tax registration.

Caisse d'amortissement: central sinking fund set up in 1799.

Caisse de service: central service fund set up in 1806 to receive taxes from the departments.

centimes additionnels: additional direct taxes, supplementing the land, industrial and commercial taxes.

commis: clerk(s) of lower grade in public service.

conseils d'administration: advisory administrative councils which served each minister.

Cour des comptes: central accounts office set up in 1807 to audit state finances.

cours d'appel: name given to the appeal tribunals in 1804 and changed to '*cours impériales*' (Imperial courts) in 1810.

121

cours d'assises: departmental criminal tribunals.

cultivateurs: working farmers of a sort usually denoting commoner origins but some proprietary means.

curés: priests nominated to the chief towns of cantons who alone were assured of tenure within the concordatory church.

desservants: priests in charge, but without tenure, serving at their bishops' pleasure.

Direction du recouvrement des impositions directes: office set up in each department in 1799 for the collection of the direct taxes.

Directions générales: the various internal departments of the central ministry of the interior.

Domaine extraordinaire: special fund set up early in 1810 to manage the indemnities, confiscations and other exactions levied in the conquered states.

donataires: recipients of Imperial land-gifts.

dotations: Imperial land-gifts [see also *majorats*, below].

douaniers: customs officials.

droits réunis: consolidated duties on various consumer goods which were controlled by a central excise office (*Régie*) as from 1804.

écoles centrales: standardised secondary schools established by the National Convention in 1795 and replaced by the *lycées* in 1802.

écuyers: officers of the non-titled military nobility under the old regime, roughly equivalent to English equerries.

foncière, la: the basic land tax.

'franc de germinal': the bimetallic standard adopted in March 1803 which fixed the silver content of the franc piece and the official ratio of gold to silver at 1:15.5.

livre tournois: the official unit of currency used in France until the adoption of the silver franc in 1795.

lycées: the regular secondary schools (established in each court of appeal) which replaced the *écoles centrales* in 1802.

'machine infernale': the bomb (barrel filled with powder) which exploded in the Rue Saint-Nicaise on Christmas Eve 1800, narrowly missing Napoleon.

majorats: Imperial land-gifts which were granted the status of heritable (entailed) estates.

'Négociants réunis': the financial group led by Ouvrard in 1804–6 whose aim was to ship Spanish American bullion (piastres) into France via Spain, and whose collapse precipitated the Bank panic of 1805–6.

notables: specifically, those whose names appeared on the Napoleonic electoral lists; generally, those who mattered in Imperial society.

octroi: consumer duties (*droits d'octroi*) levied on certain goods entering the large cities of France.

officiers: royal office-holders of the old regime.

partage: the procedure officially adopted during the Revolution to allow the division of estates among all male heirs in place of the rights of primogeniture.

patente, la: small direct tax on trades and commercial services.

pays alliés: the nominally sovereign states allied with France.

pays conquis: the conquered territories which formed the subject states of France.

pays réunis: non-French territories directly annexed to France.

personnelle-mobilière, la: direct tax on personal or industrial incomes.

'personnes les plus marquantes': lists of the 60 to 80 'most distinguished' persons in each department drawn up in the later years of the Empire.

'plus imposés': the highest taxpayers in each department, from among whom the members of the departmental electoral colleges *had* to be chosen as from August 1802.

'ralliés': those who 'rallied' to Napoleon, either at the time of Brumaire or later; his open supporters.

rentiers: stock-holders; persons of independent means.

senatus-consultum: procedure (first adopted in January 1801) empowering the senate, by the rights vested in it of preserving and amending the constitution, to announce its sanction of major constitutional changes and other laws Napoleon wished to introduce independently of the legislative body.

Select Bibliography

This list is confined to studies referred to in the text, plus a few useful reference works. Full and up-to-date bibliographies for the Napoleonic period appear in [13] and [32]. For the sake of thematic continuity, accounts of the Revolutionary background to the Consulate and Empire are included in the relevant sections of the Napoleonic bibliography below. Wherever possible, translations are cited under their English titles, along with the publication dates of the original works.

A selection of printed primary sources

[1] M.-M.-C. Gaudin, *Mémoires, souvenirs, opinions et écrits du duc de Gaëte, ancien ministre des finances*, 2 vols (1826, 1926). Should be read in conjunction with [59].

[2] J.C. Herold, *The Mind of Napoleon: A Selection from his Written and Spoken Words* (1955). A fascinating selection on many subjects covering different periods of Napoleon's life.

[3] E. de Las Cases, *Mémorial de Sainte Hélène: Journal of the Private Life and Conversations of the Emperor Napoleon at Saint Helena*, 4 vols (Eng. trans., 1823, of French original, 1823). The crucial contemporary overture to the Napoleonic legend.

[4] F.-N. Mollien, *Mémoires d'un ancien ministre du Trésor public*, 4 vols (1837).

[5] Napoleon I, *Correspondance de Napoléon Ier publiée par ordre de l'empereur Napoléon III*, 32 vols (1858–69). The official, authoritative edition of Napoleon's letters. A translated sample is available in [6].

[6] *Napoleon's Letters*, selected, translated and edited by J.M. Thompson (1934, 1954). All citations in the present text are from the later (Everyman Library) edn.

[7] Napoleon I, *Lettres au comte Mollien ministre du trésor public du 16 mars 1803 au 9 juin 1815*, ed. J. Arnna (1959). A contemporary guide to financial policy.

[8] J.-J. Rousseau, *The Social Contract* (Eng. trans. by M. Cranston,

1968, of French original, 1762). The 'classic' statement on republican principles before the French Revolution.

Dictionaries, bibliographies, conference papers, reference works

[9] D. Chandler, *Dictionary of the Napoleonic Wars* (1979). A reliable
standard reference work.

[10] O. Connelly (ed.), *Historical Dictionary of Napoleonic France, 1799–1815*
(1985). The best work of its kind in English.

[11] F. de Dainville and J. Tulard, *Atlas administratif de l'Empire français*
(1973). A series of detailed maps on all administrative aspects of
the Napoleonic Empire, with commentary in an accompanying
handbook.

[12] J. Godechot, *Les institutions de la France sous la Révolution et
l'Empire* (1951, 3rd rev. edn, 1985). The standard reference work
on institutional history from the end of the old regime to the fall
of the Empire.

[13] J.A. Meyer, *An Annotated Bibliography of the Napoleonic Era. Recent
Publications, 1945–1985* (1987).

[14] *Revue d'Histoire moderne et contemporaine*, XVII (1970), special no.
entitled 'La France à l'époque napoléonienne'. Publishes the
proceedings of the important conference held at the Sorbonne in
October 1969 to mark the bicentenary of Napoleon's birth. Most
of the papers also appear in the *Annales historiques de la Révolution
française*, XLII (1970).

[15] J. Tulard and others, *Dictionnaire Napoléon* (1987). The most
up-to-date Napoleonic dictionary in French.

Historiography and general textbooks

[16] L. Bergeron, *France under Napoleon* (Eng. trans., 1981, of French
original, 1972). Much the best of the general works on political,
social and economic structures, as well as on the 'mentalities' of
the period. Deals with domestic history. Supplemented by [25],
in its French series, on foreign aspects.

[17] É. Bourgeois, *Manuel historique de politique étrangère*, 4 vols (1906–32).
The most detailed statement on the 'oriental mirage' in Napoleon's
ambition.

[18] I. Collins, *Napoleon: First Consul and Emperor of the French* (Historical Association pamphlet, 1986). Useful, short and up-to-date
historiographical review.

[19] O. Connelly, *The Epoch of Napoleon* (1972). The best of the short
American textbooks.

[20] —— , *French Revolution/Napoleonic Era* (1979). Good on thematic

continuity or change over the period 1789–1815. Has a detailed bibliographical essay.

[21] É. Driault, *Napoléon et l'Europe*, 5 vols (1917–1927). Elaborates the theme of a 'Roman ideal' in Napoleon's ambition.

[22] P. Geyl, *Napoleon: For and Against* (1949, 1965, 1976, 1982, 1986). Still the best historiographical survey from 1815 to the Second World War, though it deals only with French writers.

[23] J. Godechot, *La Grande Nation. L'Expansion révolutionnaire de la France dans le monde 1789–1799*, 2 vols (1956, 1983). A seminal work. Detailed account of French political influence and territorial expansion during the Revolutionary decade.

[24] G. Lefebvre, *Napoleon*, 2 vols (Eng. trans., 1969 and 1974, of French original, 1965 edn). Though parts of it are now dated, this comprehensive work remains an important source.

[25] J. Lovie and A. Palluel-Guillard, *L'Épisode napoléonien: Aspects extérieurs* (1972). In the same French series as [16] but much less original.

[26] J.M. McManners, 'Napoleon', in *Lectures on European History, 1789–1914: Men, Machines and Freedom* (1966). A useful general essay full of penetrating insights.

[27] F. Markham, *Napoleon* (1963). The best of the long-serving English textbooks.

[28] F. Masson, *Napoléon et sa famille (1769–1821)*, 13 vols (1897–1919). Much the fullest treatment of the subject. Argues the case for a Corsican 'clan spirit' in Napoleon's dealings with his family.

[29] H. Rössler, *Napoleons Griff nach der Karlskrone. Das Ende des alten Reiches 1806* (1957). The clearest account of the 'Carolingian' analogy in Napoleon's ambition.

[30] A. Sorel, *L'Europe et la Révolution française*, 8 vols (1885–1904). A major pioneering work. Vol. I (Eng. trans., 1969) is good on eighteenth-century statecraft.

[31] A. Thiers, *History of the Consulate and the Empire of France under Napoleon*, 20 vols (Eng. trans., 1845–62, of French original, 1845–69). Elaborates the idea of a 'universal empire' in Napoleon's ambition. A highly sympathetic narrative much influenced by the Napoleonic legend.

[32] J. Tulard, *Napoleon: The Myth of the Saviour* (Eng. trans., 1984, of French original, 1977). The fullest of the modern 'revisionist' accounts, but the translation is often poor. Very detailed bibliography.

The Napoleonic civil state

Government, police, 'ralliés' and opposition

[33] E.A. Arnold Jr, *Fouché, Napoleon, and the General Police* (1979). Places Fouché's work in its ministerial context. Also covers the underworld of police operations.

[34] S. Balayé, *Mme de Staël: Lumières et Liberté* (1979). Deals with a celebrated writer who fell foul of Napoleon. Useful source for early French Romanticism. English readers can cover some of the same ground in [44].

[35] L. Bergeron, *La statistique en France de l'époque napoléonienne* (1981). A critical guide to the uses and pitfalls of the massive statistical data of the Napoleonic regime.

[36] C.H. Church, *Revolution and Red Tape: The French Ministerial Bureaucracy 1770–1850* (1981). Stresses the continuity of administrative personnel. Ch. 8 deals with the Napoleonic bureaucracy.

[37] H. Cole, *Fouché, the Unprincipled Patriot* (1971).

[38] I. Collins, *Napoleon and his Parliaments 1800–1815* (1979). A readable account of the personnel and procedures of the Napoleonic legislative body, tribunate, senate and electoral colleges. Extensive quotations from primary sources.

[39] C. Durand, *Le fonctionnement du Conseil d'état napoléonien* (1954). An authoritative if rather technical study.

[40] —— , *Les Auditeurs au Conseil d'état de 1803 à 1814* (1958). A basic secondary source for the training of Napoleon's administrators.

[41] J. Godechot, *Les constitutions de la France depuis 1789* (1970, 1975). A standard guide to the texts of successive constitutions in France.

[42] E. d'Hauterive (ed.), *La police secrète du Premier Empire: Bulletins quotidiens adressés par Fouché à l'Empereur, 1804–1810*, 5 vols (1908–64). Important annotated source for problems of law and order (notably military conscription).

[43] —— , *Napoléon et sa police* (1943).

[44] J.C. Herold, *Mistress to an Age: A Life of Mme de Staël* (1958). A readable biography for those who do not have the language for [34].

[45] R.B. Holtman, *The Napoleonic Revolution* (1967, 1978). Probably the best account in English of Napoleon's reforms.

[46] A. Ollivier, *Le dix-huit brumaire* (1959). A detailed study of Napoleon's *coup d'état*.

[47] B. Panagiatopoulos, 'Les structures d'âge du personnel de l'Empire', *Revue d'Histoire moderne et contemporaine*, XVII (1970). A short but important communication of primary research.

[48] F. Ponteil, *Napoléon Ier et l'organisation autoritaire de la France* (1956, 1965). Still useful on the principles and structures of the Napoleonic state.

[49] J. Savant, *Les préfets de Napoléon* (1958). Should be read in conjunction with [50].

[50] —— , *Les ministres de Napoléon* (1959). Better on the men than on their official functions, as is [49].

[51] M.S. Staum, 'The Class of Moral and Political Sciences, 1795–1803', *French Historical Studies*, XI (Spring, 1980).

[52] J. Thiry, *Le Sénat de Napoléon, 1800–1814* (1932). A standard work.

[53] E.A. Whitcomb, 'Napoleon's Prefects', *American Historical Review*, LXXIX (1974).

[54] —— , *Napoleon's Diplomatic Service* (1979). Like [53], a pro-sopographic analysis, with important conclusions.

Finance

[55] F. Aftalion, *L'économie de la Révolution française* (1987). The most detailed modern account of the monetary disorder caused by the assignats. Useful for background to Napoleon's reforms.

[56] J.F. Bosher, *French Finances 1770–1795: From Business to Bureaucracy* (1970). Deals mainly with financial institutions. Some essential background for Napoleon's reforms.

[57] J. Bouvier, 'A propos de la crise dite de 1805: Les crises économiques sous l'Empire', *Revue d'Histoire moderne et contemporaine*, XVII (1970).

[58] S.G. Harris, *The Assignats* (1930). A pioneering work. Useful for background.

[59] F. Latour, *Le grand argentier de Napoléon, Gaudin, duc de Gaëte* (1962). Should be read in conjunction with [1].

[60] M. Marion, *Histoire financière de la France depuis 1715* (1914–28), vol. IV: *1799–1818: La fin de la Révolution, le Consulat et l'Empire, la libération du territoire* (1925). A comprehensive financial history which has weathered well.

[61] M. Payard, *Le financier Ouvrard, 1770–1846* (1958). A study of economic adventurism through the career of one of its controversial practitioners.

[62] R. Schnerb, 'La dépression économique sous le directoire après la disparition du papier-monnaie (an V–an VIII), *Annales historiques de la Révolution française*, XI (1934).

[63] R. Szramkiewicz, *Les régents et censeurs de la Banque de France nommés sous le Consulat et l'Empire* (1974). A prosopographic analysis of the world of high finance under Napoleon.

[64] G. Thuillier, 'Crédit et économie sous l'Empire: Les "notes sur la banque" de Joseph Fiévée (1806)', *Revue d'Histoire économique et sociale*, XLI (1963).

[65] —— , 'Pour une histoire monétaire du XIXe siècle: La crise monétaire de l'automne 1810', *Revue historique*, CCXXXVIII (1967). Investigates a neglected detail of the French economic crisis of 1810–11.

[66] —— , 'Le stock monétaire de la France en l'an X', *Revue d'Histoire économique et sociale*, LII (1974).

[67] —— , 'Pour une histoire monétaire de la France du XIXe siècle: La réforme de l'an XI', *Revue de l'Institut Napoléon*, CXXXI (1975). A study of the adoption and significance of the '*franc de germinal*' of 1803.

[68] —— , 'Les troubles monétaires en France de 1803 à 1808', ibid., CXXXIII (1977).

[69] J. Godel, *La reconstruction concordataire dans le diocèse de Grenoble après la Révolution (1802–1809)* (1968). A major regional study of the concordatory church in operation. Should be read in conjunction with [74].

[70] —— , 'L'Église selon Napoléon', *Revue d'Histoire moderne et contemporaine*, XVII (1970). An excellent digest of the main themes of [69].

[71] E.E.Y. Hales, *Napoleon and the Pope: The Story of Napoleon and Pius VII* (1962). A standard text on the rupture in Church–State relations.

[72] O. Hufton, 'The reconstruction of a church 1796–1801', in *Beyond the Terror: Essays in French Regional and Social History, 1794–1815*, ed. G. Lewis and C. Lucas (1983). Traces the religious revival in France shortly before the Concordat.

[73] H. Jedin and J.P. Dolan (eds), *History of the Church* (1965–), vol. VII: *The Church between Revolution and Restoration* (1981). Part of a long and scholarly series originally published in German.

[74] C. Langlois, *Le diocèse de Vannes au XIXe siècle, 1800–1830. Un diocèse breton au début du XIXe siècle* (1974). A major regional study of the Church and of popular religiosity. Should be read in conjunction with [69].

[75] A. Latreille, *L'Église catholique et la Révolution française*, 2 vols (1946–50). A long-serving standard text.

[76] J.M. McManners, *The French Revolution and the Church* (1969). The best general account of the Church during the Revolutionary upheavals preceding the Concordat.

[77] F. Malino, *The Sephardic Jews of Bordeaux: Assimilation and Emancipation in Revolutionary and Napoleonic France* (1978). A specialised regional study of an old Jewish community in France.

[78] D. Robert, *Les églises réformées en France 1800–1830* (1961). Deals with Napoleon's organisation of the Protestant churches.

[79] S. Schwarzfuchs, *Napoleon, the Jews and the Sanhedrin* (1979). Takes a more general approach than [77]. Covers the whole Empire and also Jewish communities beyond it.

[80] H.H. Walsh, *The Concordat of 1801: A Study of the Problem of Nationalism in the Relations of Church and State* (1933). A detailed examination of the terms and context of its subject.

Legal codes, justice, education, press, propaganda

[81] J. Bourdon, *La législation du Consulat et de l'Empire*, 2 vols (1942), vol. I: *La réforme judiciaire de l'an VIII*. Technical, but important in its field.

[82] A. Cabanis, *La presse sous le Consulat et l'Empire* (1975). Detailed coverage of censorship and police controls.

[83] R.B. Holtman, *Napoleonic Propaganda* (1950, 1968). The best work in English on the topic.

[84] H.-F. Koechlin, *Compétence administrative et judiciaire de 1800 à 1830* (1951). A technical explanation of the overlapping functions of justice and administration under Napoleon.

[85] A. Léon, 'Promesses et ambiguïtés de l'oeuvre d'enseignement technique en France de 1800 à 1815', *Revue d'Histoire moderne et contemporaine*, XVII (1970).

[86] B. Schwartz (ed.), *The Code Napoleon and the Common-Law World* (1956). A collection of eighteen essays on specialised aspects of the Code in France and abroad. See especially those by C. Léwy on property and by M. Rheinstein on the family.

Warfare and the military establishment

[87] E.A. Arnold Jr, 'Some Observations on the French Opposition to Napoleonic Conscription, 1804–1806', *French Historical Studies*, IV (Fall, 1966). Challenges the assumption that opposition to military conscription was not a serious problem before 1812.

[88] H. de la Barre de Nanteuil, *Le comte Daru, ou l'administration militaire sous la Révolution et l'Empire* (1966). A personal study set in its institutional context.

[89] M. Barthrop, *Napoleon's Egyptian Campaigns, 1798–1799* (1978). A clear, reliable account.

[90] J.-P. Bertaud, *The Army of the French Revolution: From Citizen-Soldiers to Instrument of Power* (Eng. trans., 1988, of French original, 1979). A major study of military developments in France in the 1790s. Essential background to Napoleon's rising career.

[91] ——, 'Napoleon's Officers', *Past & Present*, no. 112 (Aug. 1986). Discusses the system of honours and promotions in Napoleon's army and the social origins of his officer corps.

[92] T.C.W. Blanning, *The Origins of the French Revolutionary Wars* (1986). The best introduction in English to the subject.

[93] A.S.K. Brown (ed.), *The Anatomy of Glory: Napoleon and his Guard* (1962). Touches on the origins of the Napoleonic legend.

[94] D. Chandler, *The Campaigns of Napoleon* (1966). An informative standard text.

[95] L. Chardigny, *Les maréchaux de Napoléon* (1977, 1980). The best of many works on the marshals, especially in analysis of their social backgrounds.

[96] O. Connelly, *Blundering to Glory: Napoleon's Military Campaigns* (1988). An interesting reassessment of the subject, not always flattering to Napoleon. Well illustrated by maps.

[97] J. Houdaille, 'Pertes de l'armée de terre sous le premier Empire, d'après les registres matricules', *Population*, XXVII (1972). These careful estimates are a revision of his earlier figures for French war losses published in the *Annales historiques de la Révolution française*,

XLII (1970), and have become the current consensus. The latter source also includes a note by M. Reinhard on 'one Paris night will replace them all'.

[98] H. Lachouque, *Napoléon et la garde impériale* (1957). A readable account, also useful on the origins of the Napoleonic legend. Readers without French can consult [93].

[99] J.A. Lynn, 'Toward an Army of Honor: The Moral Evolution of the French Army, 1789–1815', *French Historical Studies*, XVI (Spring, 1989). The same issue also publishes a lively debate on the subject between the author and O. Connelly.

[100] J. Morvan, *Le soldat impérial*, 2 vols (1904). A 'classic' early study of Napoleon's rank and file.

[101] G.E. Rothenberg, *The Art of Warfare in the Age of Napoleon* (1977). Discusses many aspects of the subject. Particularly useful on military organisation.

[102] S.F. Scott, *The Response of the Royal Army to the French Revolution: The Role and Development of the Line Army 1787–1793* (1978). Covers some of the same early ground as [90]. Important for the background to Napoleon's rising military career.

[103] G. Six, *Les généraux de la Révolution et de l'Empire* (n.d. [1947]). A crucial pioneering work on Napoleon's higher officer corps.

Society and the Imperial élite

[104] L. Bergeron, G. Chaussinand-Nogaret and R. Forster, 'Les notables du "Grand Empire" en 1810', *Annales ÉSC*, XXVI/5 (1971). A study of five representative French departments.

[105] L. Bergeron and G. Chaussinand-Nogaret, *Les "masses de granit": Cent mille notables du Premier Empire* (1979). A computerised analysis of the members of the departmental and arrondissement electoral colleges of the Empire.

[106] —— (gen. eds), *Grands notables du Premier Empire*, 16 vols (1978–87). Biographical notices on the 'most distinguished' citizens of each French department (40 to date) during the later Empire. Series continuing.

[107] P. Durye, 'Les chevaliers dans la noblesse impériale', *Revue d'Histoire moderne et contemporaine*, XVII (1970).

[108] G. Ellis, 'Rhine and Loire: Napoleonic elites and social order', in *Beyond the Terror: Essays in French Regional and Social History, 1794–1815*, ed. G. Lewis and C. Lucas (1983). A historiographical review of the main themes and findings in Napoleonic social history, with communication of original material on two contrasting departments.

[109] R. Forster, 'The Survival of the Nobility during the French Revolution', *Past & Present*, no. 37 (July 1967).

[110] M. Senkowska-Gluck, 'Les donataires de Napoléon', *Revue d'Histoire moderne et contemporaine*, XVII (1970). A seminal essay on the important topic of Napoleon's land-gifts.

[111] G.V. Taylor, 'Types of Capitalism in Eighteenth-century France', *English Historical Review*, LXXIX (1964). Establishes the primacy of 'proprietary capitalism' in France before the Revolution. Of thematic importance to the period 1789–1815.

[112] —— , 'Noncapitalist Wealth and the Origins of the French Revolution', *American Historical Review*, LXXII (1967). Also important for background.

[113] J. Tulard, 'Problèmes sociaux de la France impériale', *Revue d'Histoire moderne et contemporaine*, XVII (1970).

[114] —— , 'Les composants d'une fortune: Le cas de la noblesse d'empire', *Revue historique*, CCLIII (1975).

[115] —— , *Napoléon et la noblesse d'Empire* (1979). Integrates some of the material in [113] and [114]. Publishes a full alphabetical list (by title) of the Imperial nobility. The most accessible reference work of its kind.

[116] J. Vidalenc, *Les émigrés français 1789–1825* (1963). The standard modern text on the subject. Covers Napoleon's amnesties.

Annexed lands and subject states

[117] H. Berding, *Napoleonische Herrschafts- und Gesellschaftspolitik im Königreich Westfalen 1807–1813* (1973). Important study of the social effects of Napoleon's land-gifts in a German satellite kingdom.

[118] —— , 'Le Royaume de Westphalie, État-modèle', *Francia*, X (1982). A short cut to [117]. Dispels the myth that the kingdom of Westphalia was a 'bourgeois monarchy' and a paradigm of Napoleonic reform.

[119] T.C.W. Blanning, *The French Revolution in Germany: Occupation and Resistance in the Rhineland 1792–1802* (1983). Excellent account of French policy on the German left bank of the Rhine before its definitive annexation to France.

[120] O. Connelly, *Napoleon's Satellite Kingdoms* (1965, 1969). The best general introduction to the subject.

[121] —— , *The Gentle Bonaparte: A Biography of Joseph, Napoleon's Elder Brother* (1968). A sympathetic and often moving portrait.

[122] R. Davico, *"Peuple" et notables (1750–1816). Essais sur l'Ancien Régime et la Révolution en Piémont* (1981). An important study of the impact of the French Revolution and Napoleon on Piedmont. Particularly good on social history.

[123] R. Devleeshouwer, 'Le cas de la Belgique', in *Occupants-Occupés, 1792–1815* (1969). Traces Belgian reactions to French rule over the whole period.

[124] J.M. Diefendorf, *Businessmen and Politics in the Rhineland, 1789–1834* (1980). Primarily concerned with the business élites of Cologne, Aachen and Crefeld under French and later Prussian rule.

[125] M. Dunan, *Napoléon et l'Allemagne. Le Système continental et les débuts du royaume de Bavière, 1806–1810* (1942). A major pioneering

work which unfortunately stops before the end of the Napoleonic experience.

[126] E. Fehrenbach, *Der Kampf um die Einführung des Code Napoléon in den Rheinbundstaaten* (1973). A short cut to the main lines of [127].

[127] ———, *Traditionale Gesellschaft und revolutionäres Recht. Die Einführung des Code Napoléon in den Rheinbundstaaten* (1974). The most authoritative text on the less than successful application of the *Code Napoléon* in the Rhenish Confederation.

[128] ———, 'Verfassungs- und sozialpolitische Reformen und Reform-projekte in Deutschland unter dem Einfluss des napoleonischen Frankreich', in H. Berding and H.-P. Ullmann (eds), *Deutschland zwischen Revolution und Restauration* (1981). A more general survey than [127], but has a similar conclusion.

[129] A. Fugier, *Napoléon et l'Italie* (1947). An old general text which can still be read with profit.

[130] 'L'Italie jacobine et napoléonienne', special no. of the *Annales historiques de la Révolution française*, XLIX (1977). An important set of articles by recognised specialists on various aspects of French rule in Italy from the 1790s to 1815.

[131] G.H. Lovett, *Napoleon and the Birth of Modern Spain*, 2 vols (1965). A scholarly, readable and reliable account of a subject not otherwise well served by English works. Good on the origins of Spanish nationalism in the war for independence.

[132] *Occupants-Occupés, 1792–1815. Colloque de Bruxelles, 29 et 30 janvier 1968* (1969). A collection of conference papers on certain subject lands under French rule or military occupation. A broad, thematic approach.

[133] S. Schama, *Patriots and Liberators: Revolution in the Netherlands 1780–1813* (1977). A stimulating account with detailed coverage of the impact of the French Revolution and Napoleon on Holland.

[134] C. Schmidt, *Le grand-duché de Berg (1806–1813). Étude sur la domination française en Allemagne sous Napoléon Ier* (1905). In its time a 'model' study of a German state under French rule. Methodologically influential, and covers all aspects.

[135] M. Senkowska-Gluck, 'Les majorats français dans le duché de Varsovie (1807–1813)', *Annales historiques de la Révolution française*, XXXVI (1964). A useful short cut to her detailed work in Polish on the French land-gifts in the duchy of Warsaw.

[136] ———, 'Le duché de Varsovie', in *Occupants-Occupés, 1792–1815* (1969). Takes a wider view than [135].

[137] J. Suratteau, 'Occupation, occupants et occupés en Suisse de 1792 à 1814', in *Occupants-Occupés, 1792–1815* (1969). The most detailed contribution to [132]. Valuable source.

[138] P. Villani, *Mezzogiorno tra riforme e rivoluzione* (1962). A broad sweep across the period 1734–1860. Concentrates on the kingdom of Naples.

[139] ———, *La vendita dei beni dello Stato nel regno di Napoli (1806–1815)*

(1964). A specialised monograph on the land sales in the kingdom of Naples. Important conclusions.

[140] P. Villani, *Italia napoleonica* (1978). A short textbook which reviews the main conclusions of [138] and [139] in the light of Napoleon's impact on Italy as a whole.

[141] S. Woolf, *A History of Italy 1700–1860: The Social Constraints of Political Change* (1979). Has important chapters on the effects of the French Revolution and Napoleon in Italy. The best English work on the theme of its sub-title.

The Imperial economy and Continental Blockade

[142] L. Bergeron, 'Problèmes économiques de la France napoléonienne', *Revue d'Histoire moderne et contemporaine*, XVII (1970). A survey of the state of the sources twenty years ago.

[143] ——, 'Remarques sur les conditions du développement industriel en Europe occidentale à l'époque napoléonienne', *Francia*, I (1973). Good on the inland aspects.

[144] ——, *Banquiers, négociants et manufacturiers parisiens du Directoire à l'Empire* (1978). A vital work. The most authoritative account of the financial, commercial and industrial élite in France at that time.

[145] P. Butel, 'Crise et mutation de l'activité économique à Bordeaux sous le Consulat et l'Empire', *Revue d'Histoire moderne et contemporaine*, XVII (1970). Also examines the social consequences of economic dislocation.

[146] ——, 'Guerre et commerce: L'activité du port de Bordeaux sous le régime des licences, 1808–1815', ibid., XIX (1972). Qualifies earlier accounts through chronological distinctions and by an analysis of various economic sectors.

[147] F. Crouzet, 'les importations d'eaux-de-vie et de vins français en Grande-Bretagne pendant le Blocus continental', *Annales du Midi*, LXV (1953).

[148] ——, *L'Économie britannique et le Blocus continental (1806–1813)*, 2 vols (1958) (new edn, 1988). The definitive work on this hitherto neglected subject. Has a pithy general conclusion.

[149] ——, 'Les conséquences économiques de la Révolution', *Annales historiques de la Révolution française*, XXXIV (1962). Publishes and analyses a text by Sir Francis d'Ivernois.

[150] ——, 'Wars, Blockade, and Economic Change in Europe, 1792–1815', *Journal of Economic History*, XXIV (1964). An important seminal essay which extends the coverage of [149] thematically over the whole period of the French wars.

[151] ——, *De la supériorité de l'Angleterre sur la France. L'économique et l'imaginaire XVIIe–XXe siècles* (1985). A collection of articles which republishes [149] and a French version of [150], along with some others relevant to Napoleonic economic history. Excellent bibliographical endnotes.

[152] F. Crouzet, and others (eds), *Essays in European Economic History 1789–1914* (1969). See especially the essays by J. Dhondt on the cotton industry at Ghent during the French regime and by G. Adelmann on the Rhenish linen and cotton trades at the outset of industrialisation.

[153] R. Devleeshouwer, 'Le Consulat et l'Empire: Période de "take-off" pour l'économie belge?', *Revue d'Histoire moderne et contemporaine*, XVII (1970).

[154] G. Ellis, *Napoleon's Continental Blockade: The Case of Alsace* (1981). Stresses the importance of the inland dimension and of the French continental market design in Napoleon's economic policies. Has a full bibliography on the Blockade.

[155] W.F. Galpin, *The Grain Supply of England during the Napoleonic Period* (1925). A long-serving text.

[156] E.F. Heckscher, *The Continental System: An Economic Interpretation* (Eng. trans., 1922, of Swedish original, 1919). For many years the standard general text on the subject. Influenced by liberal economic ideas and is generally critical of the Blockade's aims and effects. Should be read in conjunction with [154].

[157] W.O. Henderson, *Britain and Industrial Europe 1750–1870: Studies in British Influence on the Industrial Revolution in Western Europe* (1954, 1965). An informative reference work on the 'export' of industrial technology.

[158] P. Jeulin, *L'Évolution du port de Nantes. Organisation et trafic depuis les origines* (1929).

[159] B. de Jouvenel, *Napoléon et l'économie dirigée. Le Blocus continental* (1942). Combines some interesting ideas with too much uncritical quotation and some bland over-simplifications.

[160] J. Labasse, *Le commerce des soies à Lyon sous Napoléon et la crise de 1811* (1957). Takes a short-term view of the economic fluctuations of the silk industries in Lyons, and is rather too pessimistic about the Blockade's effects there.

[161] M. Lévy-Leboyer, *Les banques européennes et l'industrialisation internationale dans la première moitié du XIXe siècle* (1964). A detailed and authoritative account of the interrelationships between finance, industry and trade. Very good on the structure and working of capital markets.

[162] P. Masson, 'Marseille depuis 1789: Marseille et Napoléon', *Annales de la Faculté des Lettres d'Aix*, XI/1–4 (1917–18).

[163] F.E. Melvin, *Napoleon's Navigation System. A Study of Trade Control during the Continental Blockade* (1919). A rather unbalanced account, though typical of earlier Blockade studies in English. Argues that Napoleon's 'navigation system' was a major key to his rule, but does not cover the wider inland aspects adequately.

[164] M. Tacel, 'La place de l'Italie dans l'économie impériale de 1806 à 1814', in M. Dunan (ed.), *Napoléon et l'Europe* (1961). A perceptive short survey of the Blockade's effects on agriculture in the subject states of Italy and of the importance of some local military markets there.

135

[165] E. Tarlé, *Le Blocus continental et le royaume d'Italie. La situation économique de l'Italie sous Napoléon Ier* (1931). A detailed regional study by a prolific Blockade historian. Its conclusions need revision in the light of more recent research – e.g. the essay by Villani in [130].

[166] A. Thépot, 'Le Système continental et les débuts de l'industrie chimique en France', *Revue de l'Institut Napoléon*, no. 99 (Apr. 1966). Short, pithy, reliable.

[167] O. Viennet, *Napoléon et l'industrie française. La crise de 1810–1811* (1947). For many years a standard account of the crisis, but does not adequately explain the problem of over-stocking and over-production in 1810–11.

Collapse of Empire and Napoleonic legend

[168] R. Alexander, 'The *Fédérés* of Dijon in 1815', *Historical Journal*, XXX (1987). Covers a neglected topic. Interesting on 'popular Bonapartism' during the Hundred Days.

[169] F. Bluche, *Le plébiscite des Cent-Jours* (1974). Establishes the high abstentions in the plebiscite on the 'Additional Act' of 1815.

[170] —— , *Le Bonapartisme aux origines de la droite autoritaire, 1800–1850* (1980). A good attempt to deal with an elusive subject. Sets the legend against the record, and has some political spine.

[171] H. Lachouque, *Napoléon en 1814* (1959). A readable account of the events leading to the first abdication.

[172] H.T. Parker, 'Napoleon's Changing Self-image to 1812: A Sketch', *Proceedings of the [1983] Consortium on Revolutionary Europe* (Athens, Ga., 1985). A perceptive synopsis of his earlier work on the formation of Napoleon's personality.

[173] J.M. Sherwig, *Guineas and Gunpowder. British Foreign Aid in the Wars with France 1793–1815* (1969). A definitive account which dispels the myth of British largesse for most of the period, but also shows the high concentration of subsidies to the Allies in 1813–15. Good on the costs of the Peninsular War and on Russia's role in the Sixth Coalition.

For other aspects of the Napoleonic legend, [3] is essential, and [93] and [98] are useful.

Index

Aachen, 86
administration: civil, **19–28**, 48–9;
  military, **54–64**; *see also* army,
  French
administrative councils, 20, 25
Adriatic, 52, 53
agriculture, 94–5, 105
Ajaccio, 8
Alexander I, 52, 71, 107
allied states (of France), 62, 83
Alps, 15, 87
amalgame (1793), 60
Amiens, Peace of (1802), 30, 43, 96
amnesties (1800 and 1802), 29, 74;
  see also nobility, old regime
Amsterdam, 104
Andréossy, 92
annexed territories, 14, 15–16, 37,
  62, 70, **82–7**, 102
army, French: artillery reserve, 62;
  Brumaire, *see* Brumaire coup;
  careerism, 9, 11–12, 29, 55;
  cavalry reserve, 62; commissary
  general, 62; conscription, 43,
  59–62; corps, 65, 66–7;
  desertion and draft evasion,
  63–4; emigrations (1790s), 9;
  Fructidor (1797), 11; general
  staff, 62; 'Grand Army', 12, 50,
  54, 55, 58, 67, 70: size of, 61–2;
  'Guards of Honour', 62;
  'Honour', 'honours' and
  'Virtue', 58–9; Imperial Guard,
  62, 66, 67; 'living off the land',
  16, 70; *Maison*, 62; military
  divisions, 55, 82–3, 85; officer
  promotion, 58; officers' social
  origins, 55–8;

provisioning contracts, 61; 'sub-
  stitutes', 60;
  training, 63; transport, 62–3, 65;
  under Restoration, 110;
  Vendémiaire (1795), 10, 11;
  weapons, 64, 65; *see also*
  administration, military
Arnold, 63–4
Arrighi, 115
arrondissements, 20, 26, 44
arts, 32–3
Aspern-Essling, battle of (1809), 69
assignats, 16, 33, 37
Auerstädt, battle of (1806), 51, 68
Augereau, 11, 12, 56, 92, 115
Austerlitz, battle of (1805), 50,
  63, 68, 112–13
Austria, 9, 51, 68, 70, 71, 78, 92
Austrian marriage (1810), 53, 76
Avignon, 14, 108

Bacciochi, 51, 114, 115
Baden, grand duchy of, 31, 83, 89
Baltic, 53, 99, 100, 105
Bank of France, 37–8, 79, 111
Barbé-Marbois, 33, 36, 115
Barras, 10
Barthélemy, 11
Batavian Republic, 14, 51
Bauwens, 103
Bavaria, kingdom of, 83, 89
Baylen, capitulation of (1808), 71
Beauregard, Treaty of (1800), 43
Belgium, 14, 16, 55, 84, 85, 102,
  103, 108, 111
Berding, 90–1
Berg, grand duchy of, 52, 83,
  89–90, 105–6

137

Bergeron, 2, 3, 6, 39, 77, 78, 81, 94, 98, 106
Berlin decree (1806), 96
Bernadotte, 12, 53, 56, 90, 114, 115
Bertaud, 57–8
Berthier, 12, 54, 56, 62, 68, 75, 90, 114, 115, 118
Berthollet, 103
Bessières, 12, 56, 115
biens communaux, 38
biens nationaux, 13–14, 29, 74, 86, 87, 88, 101
Bigot de Préameneu, 115
Blanning, 4
Bologna, 15
Bonaparte, Carlo, 8
Bonaparte, Caroline, 52, 114, 115
Bonaparte, Élisa, 51, 114, 115
Bonaparte, Jérôme, 52, 90, 91, 114, 115
Bonaparte, Joseph, 51, 52, 69, 71, 88, 114, 115, 118
Bonaparte, Louis, 51, 114, 116, 118
Bonaparte, Lucien, 18
Bonaparte, Napoleon: abdication (first), 20, 78, 107: (second), 67, 108; ambition, 6–7, 53–4; campaigns and battles, *see under specific names*; 'Carolingian' analogy, 6–7; charisma, 112–13; commander-in-chief, 54, 67–8; coronation (1804), 6, 42, 50; *coup d'état, see* Brumaire coup; emperor (1804), 20, 50; first consul (1799), 19, 20, 23, 25–6, 41; 'grand strategy', 69–72; in historiography, 1–7, 113; liberal critics of, 31–3; life consulate (1802), 20, 22, 31; military career to 1799, 8–12; Napoleonic legend, 6, 67, 108, 110, 113; relations with family, 9; social reformer, 82, 83, 92–3, 111; tactics and strategy, 64–9; *see also* warfare, Napoleonic
Bonaparte, Pauline, 79, 90, 92, 116
Bordeaux, 27, 96, 100–1
Borghese, 116, 118

Borodino, battle of (1812), 69, 71
Boulogne camp, 61, 69, 97
Bourgeois (historian), 6
Bremen, 53, 104, 105
Brumaire coup (1799), 11, 12, 18, 19, 40, 78
Brune, 12, 56, 116
Brunswick, 52
Butel, 100

Cadoudal conspiracy, 30
Caisse d'amortissement, see sinking fund
Caisse de garantie, 36
Caisse de service, see service fund
Cambacérès, 19, 116, 118
Campo Formio, Treaty of (1797), 10
cantons, 20, 26, 41; assemblies of, 21, 23
capitalism (proprietary), 13
Caprara, 42
'careers open to talents', 27, 49, 58, 76
Carnot, 11
Castlereagh, 107
Catechism, Imperial, 46, 112
Caulaincourt, 116
censorship, 32
centimes additionnels, 26, 34
Champagny, 116
Chandler, 61
Chaptal, 24, 103, 116
Charlemagne, 6
Charles IV (Spain), 52
Charles XIII (Sweden), 53
Chateaubriand, 48
Chaussinand-Nogaret, 77, 78, 81
Church: Civil Constitution of the Clergy (1790), 13, 39, 43; Concordat (1801), 29, 39–44, 47, 73, 84, 111; land sales, 13, 39, 40, 45, 73, 74, 84; ordinations, 43; '*Petite Église*', 40; rupture in Church-State relations, 42
Cisalpine Republic, 15, 87
Cispadane Republic, 15
Civil Code, 45–6, 73–4, 84; *see also Code Napoléon*

138

Civil Constitution of the Clergy, *see* Church
Clarke, 55, 116
Coalitions (Allied), 52, 66, 72, 107
Code Napoléon, 45, 83, 84; in Rhenish Confederation, 89–91; in duchy of Warsaw, 91–2; *see also* Civil Code
codes (of French Empire), 5–6, 46, 83, 84, 85, 87, 88, 93, 110, 111
Collins, 4
Cologne, 86
colonies, French, 108; trade with, 16, 96
communes, 20, 26–7
Concordat, *see* Church
Connelly, 3–4, 68
Consalvi, 40
Constant, 31, 107–8
Constituent Assembly, *see* National (Constituent) Assembly
Constitutions: of 1791, 18; of 1793, 18; of the Year III (1795), 10, 18–19; of the Year VIII (1799), **19–23**, 26, 30; of the Year X (1802), 20, 23, 31; of the Year XII (1804), 20; Additional Act to (1815), 107–8
Consulate: annexations during, 15, 50; constitutions (1799–1804), 19–23, 30, 31
consuls, 19, 22, 23
Continental Blockade, 4, 5, 42, 52, 70, 111; aims of, **95–9**; effects of, **99–106**; *see also* Continental System
Continental System, 5, 95; *see also* Continental Blockade
coronation, *see* Bonaparte, Napoleon
corps, *see* army, French
Corsica, 8–9
council of ancients, 19, 28
council of 500, 18, 19, 28
council of state, 20–1, 22, 23–4, 31, 55; auditors attached to, 27, 28
Cour des comptes, 36

courts, *see* justice
Crefeld, 86
Crétet, 38, 116
Crouzet, 96, 106
customs, 12, 13, 83; and smuggling, 99–100, 105

Daru, 55, 116
Davico, 86–7
Davout, 12, 55, 56, 68, 92, 110, 116
Decrès, 116
Dejean, 55, 116
Delambre, 34
departmental councils, 20, 26
departments, 16, 20, 25–6, 50, 53; *see also* prefects and prefectures
Diefendorf, 86
Directory (1795–9), 2, 10, 11, 16, 18–19, 28, 29, 33, 35, 39, 46, 59
Domaine extraordinaire, 35, 38, 53, 55, 91; *see also* war indemnities
donataires, 77, 79, 90–1, 92; total number, 81, 114
dotations, *see* land-gifts, Imperial
Doyle, 4
Driault, 6
droits réunis, 34–5
Dubois, 25
Ducos, 19
Dufresse, 36
Dunan, 6–7
Duroc, 92, 116
Du Teil brothers, 64

Eckmühl, battle of (1809), 68
École Normale Supérieure, 47
École Spéciale Militaire, 63
écoles centrales, 46, 47
economic crisis (1810–11), 53, 103–5
education, **48–8**
Egyptian campaign (1798–9), 11, 12, 67, 69
Elbe, 52
electoral colleges, 21, 23, 77, 81
élites, *see notables*
émigrés, *see* nobility, old regime

Empire, First: constitution (1804), 20; departments, 4, 50, 53; economy, **94–106**; population, 4, 53; proclamation, 4, 20, 22, 50, 77; *see also* 'Grand Empire'
Empire, Second, 3, 110
Enghien, 30–1
Etruria, kingdom of, 51
Eugène de Beauharnais, 51, 87, 98, 114, 115, 118
excise, *see droits réunis*
Eylau, battle of (1807), 52

'federations', (1815), 108
Fehrenbach, 89–90
Ferdinand VII (Spain), 52
Ferrara, 15
Fesch, 116
feudal (seigneurial) dues: in France, 74, 84; in Italy, 87, 88; in Westphalia, 91
feudalism: in France, 12, 13, 83–4, 93; in annexed lands and subject states, 84, 89–90, 92–3, 110–11
finances, ministry of, 33, 35, 36
financial crisis (1805–6), 35–6
financial reforms, **33–9**
Fontainebleau, 42, 63; decree (1810), 104–5
Fontanes, 48
Forster, 74, 77, 81
Fouché, 24, 25, 63, 116
Fourcroy, 47, 48
'*franc de germinal*' (1803), 37
franchise, 18–19, 21, 22; *see also* plebiscites
Francis I (Austria), 53
Frankfurt fairs, 99
Frankfurt, grand duchy of, 89
Frederick Augustus (Saxony), 52
Frederick the Great, 65
French Revolution: administrative/judicial personnel, 26, 28, 29–30; economic and social consequences, 14, 16–17, 33, 74–5, 96, 100, 106, 109; institutional reforms, 12–13, 44, 45–6; land sales, 13–14, 39, 40, 45, 73–5, 78, 85, 94, 110; population, 14, 16; territorial expansion, 14–16; wars of, 9, 11, 12, 14–15, 16, 59, 64–6, 84

Friedland, battle of (1807), 52
Fructidor (1797), 11

Galicia, 92
Gaudin, 33–4, 116
general councils, *see* departmental councils
Geneva, 14
Genoa (port), 50
Genoa, Republic of, 8, 15
German Confederation (*Bund*) of 1815, 110–11
Germany, *see under the individual states*
Geyl, 1
Ghent, 102, 103
Girard, 116
Godechot, 28
Godel, 41–2
Gourgaud, 67
Goubion Saint-Cyr, 12, 56, 110, 116
government, *see* administration, civil
'Grand Army', *see* army, French
'grand dignitaries' of the Empire, 21, 23, 77, 79, 118
'Grand Empire': beyond France, 5, 7, 95, 98, 105; collapse of, 72; and 'Grand Army', 70; population of (1811), 53; territorial expansion, **50–4**, 77; *see also* Empire, First
'grand strategy', *see* Bonaparte, Napoleon
Great Britain, 9, 17, 103–4, 108; and Continental Blockade, 96–8, 99–100, 105; economic primacy, 106; in Napoleon's 'grand strategy', 69–70
Grenoble (diocese), 41
Gribeauval, 64
Gros-Davillier, 104
Grouchy, 56, 116

Guard, Imperial, *see* army, French
Guastalla, principality of, 79
Guibert, 64, 66

Hamburg, 53, 55, 104, 105
Hanover, 52, 53, 90
Hanse towns, 53, 87
Hargenvilliers, 60
harvests, 33, 63, 94–5, 100, 105
Helvetic Republic, 15
Herold, 3
Hesse, duchy of, 89
Hesse-Cassel, 52
Hitler, 1
Holland, 9, 39, 53, 55, 62, 70,
    100; kingdom of, 51
Holy Roman Empire (abolished,
    1806), 51, 110
hostages, law of, 29
Hufton, 39–40
Hundred Days, 33, 55, 67, 107–8
'Ideologues', 32
'Illyrian Provinces', 52
industry, *see* Continental Blockade
Institute, 32, 81
interior, ministry of, 24, 47
Italian campaigns: first (1796–7),
    12: battles of, 10; second (1800),
    78
Italy, *see under the individual states*
Italy, Kingdom of, 50–1, 55, 78,
    83, 87–8, 99
Italy, Republic of, 15, 30, 87

Jacobins and Babouvists, 29, 30
Jena, battle of (1806), 51, 70
Jews, 44
Josephine, 10–11, 42
Joubert, 16
Jourdan, 56, 88, 116
Jourdan–Delbrel Law (1798), 60
Jouvenel, 5
Junot, 52, 116
justice, 12–13, **44–6**; ministry of, 24

Kellermann, 56, 116

Lacuée de Cessac, 55, 116

Lafayette, 75
Lamennais, 43
land-gifts, Imperial, 5, 77, 79–80,
    84, 114; 'ducal grand-fiefs'
    (1806), 78–9, 114; in duchy of
    Warsaw, 91–2; in kingdom of
    Westphalia, 90–1; total value
    of, 81
Langlois, 41, 43
Lannes, 12, 56, 92, 117
Las Cases, 6, 108
Lebrun, 19, 117, 118
Lefebvre (historian), 2, 63
Lefebvre (marshal), 12, 56, 90, 92,
    117
Legion of Honour, 31, 77, 79, 80,
    112; total membership (1814),
    78, 114
Legislative Assembly (1791–2),
    12–13, 28, 84
legislative body, 21, 22, 23, 28,
    31, 61
Leipzig, battle of (1813), 56
Leipzig fairs, 99
Letizia (Madame Mère), 8, 9
Le Tourneur, 28
Lévy-Leboyer, 102
Life consulate, *see* Bonaparte,
    Napoleon
Liguria and Ligurian Republic, 15,
    50, 55, 83, 85
Lille, 38
livre tournois, 37
Lombard Republic, 15
Lombardy, 50
Louis XV, 8
Louis XVI, 94
Louis XVIII, 107, 110, 111
Lowicz, principality of, 92
Lübeck, 53
Luxemburg, 14
lycées, 47, 111
Lynn, 58–9
Lyons, 27, 38, 101, 104

Macdonald, 12, 56, 92, 110, 117
'*machine infernale*', 30
McManners, 44

Mantua, 10, 15
Marengo campaign (1800), 15, 30, 40
Maret, 25, 92, 117
Marie-Louise, 53, 107
Markham, 3
Marmont, 12, 56, 75, 110, 117
Marseilles, 27, 101, 103
marshals, 11–12, 55–6, 59, 66–7, 78, 80, 91–2, 110; *see also* army, French
Massa-Carrara, 78, 114
Masséna, 12, 56, 68, 92, 117
Masson, 9
mayors, 20, 27, 48
Melvin, 95
Melzi d'Eril, 87–8, 117
Metternich, 53
Milan decrees (1807), 96
Milan, duchy of, 15
military divisions, *see* army, French
Modena, 15
Mollien, 33, 36, 38, 117
Moncey, 56, 117
Moniteur, 25, 32; *see also* propaganda
Montalivet, 24, 117
Monte Napoleone, 79
Mortier, 12, 56, 117
Morvan, 59
Moscow, 71
Mulhouse, 103, 108
municipal councils, 20, 27
municipalities, *see* communes
Murat, 12, 52, 55, 56, 114, 117, 118

Nantes, 96, 101
Naples, kingdom of, 51, 52, 78, 83, 88–9, 114
Napoleon I, *see* Bonaparte, Napoleon
Napoleon II, *see* Rome, King of
Napoleon III, 3, 110
Napoleonic legend, *see* Bonaparte, Napoleon
Nassau, duchy of, 89
National (Constituent) Assembly (1789–91), 12–13, 28, 84

National Convention (1792–5), 10, 28, 39, 84
National Guard(s), 9, 11, 62
national lands, *see biens nationaux*
national lists, 19, 21, 22
'natural frontiers' of France, 15, 50
naval blockade, British, 96, 100
Négociants réunis, 36
Ney, 12, 56, 68, 90, 117
Nice, 14, 83
nobility, Imperial: 'ducal grand-fiefs' (1806), 78, 114; dynastic aspects, 77–8; land-gifts, 5, 77, 79–80, 84, 90–2: total value of, 81; *majorates*, 78–9, 92, 114; military component, 78, 80; old nobility in, 80; titles (March decrees, 1808), 76, 78–81, 114; total number of, 80, 114; under Restoration, 110; *see also notables*
nobility, old regime: in army, 29, 56–7; in civil state, 29, 75–7; émigré property, 13–14, 29, 45, 73–5; émigrés, 9, 29, 43, 75, 110; *see also* amnesties
'notabilities', lists of, 19, 26, 30, 77, 101
notables, **73–81**; military component, 57–8; and old nobility, 75–7; in the provinces, 81; total numbers of, 78, 81, 114; under Restoration, 110; *see also*, nobility, Imperial

octroi, 34
Oldenburg, grand duchy of, 53, 87
opposition to Napoleon, 30–2
'Organic Articles', *see* Church, Concordat
Oudinot, 12, 56, 110, 117
Ouvrard, 35–6, 38

Panagiatopoulos, 28
Papal States, 15, 42, 51, 87
Paris: army intervention in, 10, 11, 18; École Militaire, 9; economic importance, 101, 103, 104; military government, 55;

142

municipal government, 20, 27; nobility in, 74–5; population trends, 109; prefecture of police, 20, 25

Paris, first Treaty of (1814), 91: (terms) 108; second Treaty of (1815): (terms) 108

Parker, 48–9, 112

Parma, 51, 78, 114

partage, 45, 109

Parthenopean Republic, 15

Peninsular War (1807–14), 53, 68, 70–1, 107

Pérignon, 56, 117

Piacenza, 78, 114

Pichegru, 11, 30

Piedmont, 15, 50, 55, 83, 84, 85, 86–7

Pious VII, 40, 42

plebiscites, 22, 31, 107–8

plus imposés, 23, 81

Poland, 5, 53, 62, 68, 70, 77, 79, 93, 99; *see also* Warsaw, duchy of

police commissioners, 20, 27, 48

police, ministry of, 24–5, 32, 63

police, prefecture of (Paris), 20, 25

Polytechnic, 47, 63

Poniatowski, 56, 117

popular unrest, 30, 95

population trends, 16, 109

Portalis, 117

Portugal, 52, 68, 70

prefects and prefectures, 20, 25–6, 28, 47, 48, 61, 76, 82, 85, 111; *see also* departments

Pressburg, Treaty of (1805), 50

prices, 94–5, 99, 105

propaganda, 18, 32, 33, 46

Protestants, 44

Prussia, 9, 51, 52, 70; Rhine Provinces of (post-1815), 86

public debt, 38–9

Pyrenees, 15, 71

'ralliés', 29–30; old nobility among, 75–7

receivers general, 20, 35, 36, 48

receivers particular, 20, 35, 48

'recess' of German diet (1803), 51, 82

Reggio, 15

Régnier, 92, 117

Restoration (Bourbon), 101, 107, 110

Revolution, and wars of, *see* French Revolution

Rhine, Confederation of, 51–2, 82; *Code Napoléon* in, 89–91

Rhine, German left bank of, 14, 16, 50, 55, 84, 85–6, 102, 108, 111

Rhine (river), 15, 82, 83, 102, 106

Richard-Lenoir, 103

Rights of Man, 19

Roer (department), 85–6

Rössler, 7

Romagna, 15

Roman Republic, 15

Rome, 51, 55, 87; King of, 53, 107

Rothenberg, 61, 62

Rotterdam, 104

Rouen, 38

Roullet de la Bouillerie, 55, 117

Rousseau (*Social Contract*), 8

royalism, 10, 11, 13, 15, 29, 30–1, 43

Russia, 1, 52, 99; campaign of (1812), 53, 61, 63, 67, 70, 71, 107

Saint-Cloud decree (1810), 100

Saint-Cyr military school, 63

Saint-Germain military school, 63

St Helena, 6, 32, 108

'Saint Napoleon's Day', 112

salons, 11, 32

Santo Domingo, 101

Savary, 24, 117

Savona, 42

Savoy, 14, 83, 108

Saxony, kingdom of, 52, 83, 106

Schmidt, 6–7

Schönbrunn, Treaty of (1809), 51

Sébastiani, 92

secretariat of state, 20, 25

Seine, general council of, 20

senate, 19, 21, 22–3, 31, 56, 61

143

senatoriates, 31, 77
senatus-consultum, 21, 23, 31, 60, 74
Senkowska-Gluck, 91–2
separation of the powers, 22
Sérurier, 56, 117
service fund, 36
Sicily, 51
Siewierz, principality of, 92
Sieyès, 19, 22
sinking fund, 33, 38
Six (historian), 56–7
Sorbonne conference (1969), 2, 94
Sorel, 97
Soult, 12, 56, 117
Spain, 9, 68, 93, 101; kingdom
  of, 52; *see also* Peninsular War
Spanish National Assembly (1808),
  52
Staël, 32
Strasbourg, 101–2, 104
strategy, *see* Bonaparte, Napoleon
subject states, 3, 5–6, 7, 35, 38,
  45, 70, 77, 82, 83, 84, **87–93**,
  98, 105, 110–11
sub-prefects, 20, 26, 48, 61
Suchet, 12, 56, 117
Sweden, 53
Swiss Confederation, 14–15, 51
Système (John Law), 37

Tacel, 105
tactics, *see* Bonaparte, Napoleon
Talleyrand-Périgord, 75, 114, 117,
  118
taxes, 12–13, 26, **33–6**
Taylor, 13
telegraph (Chappe), 65
'territorial mandates', 37
Terror, 13, 14, 18, 59
The Hague, Treaty of (1795), 14
Thiers, 6
Thompson, 3
Tilsit, Treaties of (1807), 52, 102
Tolentino, Treaty of (1797), 10
Toulon, 10
trade, *see* Continental Blockade
Trafalgar, battle of (1805), 69, 97
treasury, ministry of, 33, 36, 38

Trentino, 51
Trianon tariff (1810), 104–5
tribunate, 21, 22, 28; 'purged'
  (1802), 31–2; abolished (1807), 31
Tulard, 2, 3, 76–7, 80–1
Tuscany, grand duchy of, 51, 55, 87
Tyrol, 51

Ulm, battle of (1805), 50, 63
University, Imperial, 47–8, 85

Valtellina, 15
Vanlerberghe, 61
Vannes (diocese), 41
Venaissin, 14, 108
Vendée, 43
Vendémiaire (1795), 10, 11
Venetia, 15, 51, 78, 114
Victor, 12, 56, 110, 117
Victor Amadeus III, 15
Vienna Congress (1814–15), 93,
  108, 110
Villani, 88–9
Vimiero, battle of (1808), 71

Wagram, battle of (1809), 51, 69
war, ministry of, 54–5, 60
war administration, ministry of,
  54–5
war dead: Peninsular War, 71;
  Russian campaign, 72; total
  (1792–1815), 108–9
war indemnities, 35, 52, 70; *see also*
  Domaine extraordinaire; imposed
  on France (1815), 108
warfare, Napoleonic, **64–72**
Warsaw, duchy of, 52, 114; in
  Napoleon's spoils system, 91–2
Waterloo, battle of (1815), 67, 69,
  107, 108
Wellington, 69, 71
Westphalia, kingdom of, 52, 63,
  83, 90–1
'whiff of grapeshot', 10
Whitcomb, 76
Wolfenbüttel, 52
Woolf, 87
Württemberg, kingdom of, 83, 89